К. Паустовский

ЗОЛОТАЯ РОЗА

Заметки о писательском труде

ИЗДАТЕЛЬСТВО ЛИТЕРАТУРЫ НА
ИНОСТРАННЫХ ЯЗЫКАХ

Москва

K. Paustovsky

THE GOLDEN ROSE

Literature in the Making

FOREIGN LANGUAGES
PUBLISHING HOUSE
Moscow

TRANSLATED FROM THE RUSSIAN BY SUSANNA ROSENBERG
EDITED BY DENNIS OGDEN

DESIGNED BY L. LAMM AND K. SIROTOV

CONTENTS

To my devoted friend
Tatyana Alexeyevna Paustovskaya

Much in this work is desultory and perhaps lacking
in clarity.

Much is open to question.

This book is not a theoretical investigation, nor
is it in any way a guide to literary craftsmanship. It
contains merely my own thoughts and personal experiences in the sphere of literature.

The vast realm of the ideological foundations of
Soviet literature is not touched upon in the book since
no differences of opinion exist among us on that score.
That our literature must be a literature of great educa-
tional value is clear to all of us.

In this work I have but dealt with the little that
opportunity afforded me to relate.

And if, even to a small degree, this work enables
the reader to grasp the essential beauties of creative
writing, it will more than repay the author for the
labour expended upon it.

KONSTANTIN PAUSTOVSKY

PRECIOUS DUST

cannot remember how I came to hear the story of Jean Chamette, the Paris dustman who earned his living by sweeping the shops of the artisans of his quarter.

Chamette lived in a shanty on the outskirts of the city. To describe his neighbourhood at length would lead the reader away from the main trend of the story. I would point out, however, that to this day the outskirts of Paris are surrounded by fortifications which, at the time this story unfolds, teemed with birds and were covered with honeysuckle and hawthorn. Chamette's shanty lay at the foot of a northern rampart, in a row with the shacks of tinkers, cobblers, garbage pickers and beggars.

If Maupassant had shown an interest in the inhabitants of these shacks I am sure he would have written many more splendid stories. Perhaps he would have added more laurels to his immortal crown. But outsiders rarely peered into these places—that is, except detectives, and these only when in search of stolen goods.

His neighbours nicknamed Chamette Woodpecker, from which it may be supposed that he was a lean, hatchet-faced fellow, perhaps with a tuft of hair, like a bird's comb, protruding from under his hat.

As a private in the army of *Napoleon le Petit* during the Mexican War, Jean Chamette had known better days. He had been lucky then, too; for at Vera Cruz he had had a bout of fever and was ordered home without having fought in a single real skirmish. The officer in command of Chamette's regiment took this opportunity to send his eight-year-old daughter Suzanne back to France.

This officer was a widower who took his little daughter with him wherever he went. But the Mexican climate was fatal for European children, and the fitful guerrilla warfare was fraught with unforeseen perils. And so for once he decided to part with the little girl and send her to his sister in Rouen.

The heat hung in a haze over the Atlantic during Chamette's crossing. Little Suzanne brooded, even the fishes darting in and out of the shimmering water failed to elicit a smile from her.

Chamette looked after the child as best he could. He felt, however, that she needed not just care, but affection. But what affection could he, ex-private of a Colonial Regiment, show to a little girl? How to entertain her? Play a game of dice? Sing a smutty soldier's song?

Yet the ice had to be broken. Every now and then Chamette caught the child's bewildered glances on himself. At last he plucked up courage and embarked on a rambling tale of his own life, recalling every detail of the fishing village on the shore of the Channel where he had lived; the quicksands, the pools left by the tide, the village chapel with its cracked bell, and his mother, attending a neighbour's heart-burns.

In these recollections Chamette saw nothing that could amuse Suzanne or make her laugh. But the girl, to his surprise, hung on his every word, even pleading with him to repeat the stories and recall fresh details.

In search of these details Chamette would strain his memory until he was no longer sure that they were true. These were not really recollections, but the faint shadows of memory, melting like wreaths of mist. It had never occurred to Chamette that he would have to dig into his dull, long-buried past.

One day faint memories of the golden rose crossed his mind. Had he actually seen that rudely carved rose of blackened gold hanging above the crucifix in the house of an old fisherwoman or heard a story about it he could not tell. Now, as he began to relate Suzanne about it, he felt almost certain that he had indeed caught a glimpse of the rose. It had glittered, he remembered, though the sun was not shining and a storm raged over the Channel. The more he thought of this rose the more distinctly he recalled how the gold gleamed beneath the low ceiling.

Everybody in the village was puzzled why the fisherwoman refused to sell her treasure, which was worth a large sum. Chamette's mother alone argued that it would be sinful to sell the golden rose. It had been given to the old woman "for luck" by her sweetheart. That was long ago—when the old woman, then a happy young girl, worked in the sardine cannery at Audierne.

"Golden roses are few in this world," Chamette's mother used to say. "But the people lucky enough to possess them are sure of happiness. And not only the owners, but all who touch the rose."

As a boy Chamette had longed for the day when fortune would smile on the old fisherwoman. But in vain. Her cottage still shook in the gales and no light relieved the sombre gloom of evening.

Chamette left the village without having seen any change in the old woman's circumstances. But in Havre a year later when he met a fellow-villager, a stoker on a mail steamer, he learnt that the old woman's son, a bearded jolly painter, had turned up unexpectedly from Paris. His presence had transformed the cottage, filling it with gaiety and plenty. Artists, they say, get lots of money for their daubing.

Once while they were sitting on deck and Chamette was combing her tousled hair with his metal comb, Suzanne asked: "Jean, will anyone ever give me a golden rose?"

"You can never tell, Susie," replied Chamette. "Maybe some loon or other will turn up and present you with one. We had an old soldier in our company who had all the luck in the world. He once picked up gold teeth on the battle-field and treated the whole company to drinks. This was in the war in Annam. The tipsy gunners started firing from a mortar for the fun of it. One of the shells landed in the crater of an extinct volcano, exploded and caused it to erupt. I'll be damned if I remember the name of the volcano. It might have been Kraka-Taka, for all I know. Some eruption it was, I tell you! Forty natives lost their lives. Just think of innocent people dying, all because of an old dental plate! Then it turned out that it was our colonel who'd lost it. The whole thing, of course, was hushed up. After all, the prestige of the army must be kept up. But were we tipsy!"

"Where did that happen?" Susie queried incredulously.

"I told you, didn't I? In Annam. That's in Indo-China, where the ocean burns with hell's fire and the jellyfish look like the lace flounces around ballet girls' skirts. And it's so damp that mushrooms grow in the soldiers' boots overnight. Let them hang me if I lie."

Although he had heard plenty of soldiers' stories Chamette had never told any himself. Not that he had any scruples about inventing things, but somehow there had been no need for it. Now to amuse Suzanne he was ready to do anything.

In Rouen, Chamette handed Suzanne over to her aunt, a tall, elderly woman with a pursed-up yellow mouth. Her dress, trimmed with black sequins, made her look like a snake in a circus. On catching sight of her, Suzanne recoiled, clinging desperately to Chamette's faded greatcoat.

"Don't be afraid," whispered Chamette, urging Susie forward. "Do you think we choose our commanders in the army? Have patience, Susie, you're a soldier lass."

Chamette walked away, looking back every now and then at the windows of the gloomy house in which Suzanne's aunt lived. He made his way through the crowded streets, listening to the measured chiming of the clocks in the little shops. In his haversack lay the crumpled blue ribbon which Susie had worn in her hair. And it smelt as sweetly as though it had been lying for a long time in a basket of violets.

Mexican fever had played havoc with Chamette's health. Having been discharged from the army without getting his sergeant's stripes he now plunged into the anxieties of civilian life.

Years passed in a monotonous struggle against poverty. He tried his hand at different jobs before settling down as a dustman in Paris. The stench of sewers and garbage dumps pursued him wherever he went. It even seemed to be carried by the light breeze blowing from the Seine and he smelt it in the bunches of moist flowers sold on the boulevards by neat old women.

The days faded into a murky nothingness, relieved only by one rosy vision that now and then broke through the gloom, bringing with it the radiance of spring—the vision of Suzanne in her worn frock. It was as though Suzanne's frock, like her ribbon, had lain long in a basket of violets.

Where was Suzanne? What had become of her? He knew that her father had died of wounds and that she was now a grown-up girl.

He had often promised himself that he would go to Rouen and find her. But he kept putting off the journey until he felt it was now too late, that Suzanne had forgotten all about him. He cursed himself for his boorishness at their parting. Why hadn't he kissed her instead of pushing her towards that old hag, her aunt, and saying, "Have patience, Susie, you're a soldier lass!"

Paris dustmen work at night. There are two reasons for this: firstly, it is at the close of the day that large quantities of garbage accumulate as a result of man's strenuous but not always effective activity; secondly, the sight and the smell of refuse must not offend the Parisians. At night-time the rats are practically the only creatures that pay any attention to the scavenger's work.

Chamette liked working in the small hours of the morning, and was even touched by their beauty, particularly when the first flecks of dawn broke over the vast city and the early morning mist settled low over the Seine.

Once, just at the hour of misty dawn, while crossing the Pont des Invalides Chamette caught sight of a girl in a pale mauve dress standing sadly at the parapet and looking down into the dark waters of the Seine.

Removing his dusty hat Chamette said: "Mademoiselle, at this hour the Seine is very cold. If you allow me, I will see you home."

"I no longer have a home," replied the girl hastily, and she turned to Chamette.

Chamette's hat fell from his hands.

"Susie!" he cried, experiencing delight and dismay at the same time. "Susie, soldier lass! My little girl! We have met, at last. You haven't forgotten me, have you? I'm Jean, Jean Erneste Chamette, ex-private of the 27th Colonial Regiment, the man who brought you to that old witch in Rouen. How beautiful you've become, Susie. Your hair, it's lovely, and I never knew how to comb it."

"Jean!" exclaimed Susie and, throwing her arms around his neck, burst into tears. "Jean, good old Jean. Of course, I remember. Jean, you're as kind as ever!"

"Kind? Nonsense!" Chamette muttered. "Tell me what's happened, *ma petite.*"

Chamette drew Suzanne towards him and did what he had hesitated to do in Rouen—passed his hand over her lustrous hair and imprinted a kiss on it. But he turned away quickly, fearing that the smell of his coat would reach Suzanne's nostrils. Suzanne clung to his shoulder.

"What's happened, little one?" Chamette repeated with concern.

Suzanne did not reply, unable to restrain her sobbing. Chamette realized that this was not the time for questions.

"I've got a place down by the old ramparts," he began hurriedly. "Quite a bit from here. There's nothing to eat, unfortunately. But you can boil some water, wash, and sleep. And you can stay as long as you want."

Suzanne spent five days at Chamette's lodgings, and for five days no brighter sun had ever risen over Paris for Chamette. All the houses, even the most dilapidated and begrimed, the gardens and even Chamette's shanty, shone in its rays like the most precious jewels.

He who has not felt his pulse quicken at the measured breathing of a sleeping girl does not know what tenderness is. Her lips had the red of moist rose petals and her lashes glistened from the tears shed during the night.

Chamette had suspected what had happened to Suzanne and he was not far from the truth. Her lover, a young actor, had betrayed her. But it needed no more than the five days which Suzanne spent with Chamette to bring about a reconciliation. And things were not set right without Chamette's help. It was he who took Suzanne's letter to her lover, an insufferable dandy, who received a lesson in good manners when he tried to press a few sous into Chamette's hand.

Soon afterwards the actor arrived in a carriage to take Suzanne away. The reconciliation was accompanied by the usual bouquet, kisses, laughter, and tears, repentance and a touch of recklessness. Suzanne was so flustered that she jumped into the carriage without even saying good-bye to Chamette. Then, remembering, she blushed and held out her hand guiltily.

"If that's the kind of life you like," Chamette muttered, "may you be happy."

"I know nothing about life," replied Suzanne, tears glistening in her eyes.

"There's nothing to be worried about, darling," said the actor in a vexed tone.

"If only someone would give me a golden rose for luck," Suzanne said and sighed. "I'm sure it would make me happy. Jean, dear, I remember the story you told me on the steamer."

"Someone may," replied Chamette. "But whoever it is it will not be that fop of yours. Excuse me, I'm a soldier. I just can't stomach fops."

The young couple exchanged glances. The actor shrugged his shoulders and the carriage started off.

Chamette went about his job as usual, collecting the rubbish at the end of the day from the shops. But after the meeting with Suzanne he no longer emptied the refuse from the jewellers' in the rubbish dump. He secretly put the sweepings in a sack and brought it home with him every night. The neighbours thought he had gone out of his mind; for few people knew that the sweepings contained a certain amount of the gold dust which dropped to the floor under the jeweller's file.

It was Chamette's secret plan to sift the dust collected from the jewellers; hoping in time to amass a tiny quantity of gold which he would then mould into a small golden rose for Suzanne and so make her happy. And, perhaps, as his mother used to say, the rose might bring happiness to many other poor folk. Who could tell? He made up his mind not to see Suzanne until the rose was finished.

Chamette kept his secret to himself, fearing that if it leaked out, it would rouse the suspicions of the police. Better keep clear of them. Maybe they would take him for a thief, lock him up in gaol, and carry away his precious dust. After all, it was not *his*.

Before he joined the army Chamette had worked as a farm-hand for the village *curé*. He knew how to winnow grain and this knowledge was useful now. He remembered how the heavy grain dropped to the ground while the chaff was swept away with the wind. And so, Chamette made a little winnowing fan, and at night would winnow the dust brought from the jewellers; his heart leaping with joy each time he caught sight of a few glittering particles at the bottom of the tray.

Much time passed before he had enough gold powder to make a mould. But when he had it at last, he delayed giving it to the jeweller to shape it into a gold rose. This was not because he had no money—any jeweller would be satisfied with a third part of the mould in return for his services. The real reason was that when the rose was ready he would have to see Susie and much as he longed for the meeting, the thought of it filled him with misgivings.

All the pent-up tenderness that was in him he had kept for Susie. But who wanted the tenderness of a horrid old scarecrow who waddled on rickety, rheumatic legs. Chamette had long noticed that most people shunned him. The sight of his gaunt, grey face with its sagging skin and bulging eyes was anything but attractive. He had a chip of a broken mirror in his shack. On rare occasions

21

he would gaze at his reflection in it and immediately hurl it away with a curse. Far better not to see himself.

When at long last the rose was ready, Chamette learnt that Suzanne had left the year before for America, never to return to Paris again—so they said. Nor did anybody know her address.

At first Chamette was even somewhat relieved at this news. But, by degrees, a great disappointment, like a piece of rusty iron, sharp and cold, cut into his breast near his heart—so near that Chamette prayed for it to pierce the weary heart and stop its beating for all time.

He no longer collected the refuse. For days now he lay silently on his bed, his face turned to the wall. Once only did he smile, pressing the sleeve of his old jacket to his eyes. None of the neighbours bothered about him—they had cares of their own. One man, however, kept watch over Chamette. This was an elderly jeweller, the one who had moulded Chamette's gold into a most delicate rose with a twig containing a little sharp-pointed bud. The jeweller visited Chamette regularly, but never brought any medicine, knowing full well that the dustman was beyond recovery.

And in fact Chamette passed away before the jeweller's eyes. He raised the dead man's head, took from under his soiled pillow the golden rose, wrapped up in a crinkled blue ribbon, and departed unhurriedly, closing the creaking door behind him. The ribbon smelt of mice.

It was late autumn. The gloom of the evening was pierced by the wind and the flicking lights of lamps. The jeweller recalled how death had transformed Chamette's face, giving it an expression at once austere and serene, almost beautiful.

"That which life denies is given by death," thought the jeweller, who was fond of platitudes.

Some time afterwards he sold the rose to an elderly, shabbily dressed man of letters, who in the jeweller's opinion was not rich enough to buy anything so costly as the golden rose. Evidently the story told by the jeweller about the origin of the rose so fascinated the writer that he decided to buy it.

This elderly writer kept a journal. And it is to this that we are indebted for the story of Jean Erneste Chamette, ex-private of the 27th Colonial Regiment.

The journal contained, among other things, this entry:

"Every minute, every chance word and glance, every thought—profound or flippant—the imperceptible beat of the human heart, and, by the same token, the fluff dropping from the poplar, the starlight gleaming in a pool—all are grains of gold dust. Over the years, we writers subconsciously collect millions of these tiny grains and keep them stored away until they form a mould out of which we shape our own particular golden rose—a story, novel, or poem. From these precious particles a stream of literature is born.

"For me the story of Chamette's golden rose is symbolic of literature in the making. And just as the golden rose of the old dustman was to bring happiness to Suzanne, so with our writing. It should play its part in ensuring that beauty, the pursuit of happiness, joy and freedom, generosity and reason dissipate the gloom and shine with the brilliance of the unsetting sun."

INSCRIPTION ON A ROCK

"The writer's joy is complete
only when he is convinced that
his own conscience is in accord
with that of his fellows."

SALTYKOV-SHCHEDRIN

 remember living one winter in a seaside
cottage on the Baltic dunes. Heavy snow
lay all along the shore. And from the stately pines, too, snow was wafted down in
fluffy strands by the wind and by the frisky
little squirrels which, when it was very still,
could be heard nibbling at the cones.

The sea was only a few yards away. To reach it I
would walk down a little path past an empty cottage with
curtained windows. Fluttered by the wind, which pene-
trated through various chinks, the curtains gave me the
feeling that they were being drawn by someone who was
furtively watching my movements.

The snow, patted with rabbit tracks, extended to the
very edge of the water but the sea itself was unfrozen.

24

In stormy weather one heard not so much the roar of the surf as the crunching of ice and the rustling of settling snow. The Baltic shores are bleak and desolate in winter. The Latvians have christened the Baltic "Amber Sea" (Dzintara Jūra), and they have done so, I think, not only because it casts up much amber, but because its waters have a yellowish amber tint.

All day long a thick mist lay low on the horizon, blurring the shoreline. Here and there the gloom was relieved by white sheets of shaggy snow.

Sometimes wild geese, which that year returned too early, settled in the water and gabbled interminably. Their cries were borne to the shore, but met with no response, for in winter the coastal woods have hardly any bird life.

By day, life in the little cottage where I lived was commonplace enough. The logs crackled in the painted tile stoves, the click of my typewriter cut through the silence and Lilya, my taciturn housekeeper, sat with her knitting in the cosy hall. But with the approach of evening a mysterious atmosphere descended on the place. In the pitch dark, the tall pines pressed in upon the cottage. And the gloom of the wintry night and the solitary sea seemed to advance and engulf me the moment I stepped out of the brightly lit hall into the darkness.

The sea stretched for hundreds of miles into the black, leaden distance, without the flicker of a light or a ripple anywhere—a misty vacancy on the extremity of which stood our little cottage like a lighthouse. This was land's end. I thought how strangely the tranquil gleaming lights in the cottage, the playing of the radio, the soft carpets muffling the sound of footsteps, the open books lying on the table contrasted with the vast forbidding emptiness outside!

To the west, in the direction of Ventspils, behind the wall of black fog, lay a little fishing village. It was a very ordinary village with the nets hung out to dry, and low-roofed cottages with smoke curling from the chimneys, with trustful, long-haired dogs, and black motorboats lying on the beach.

Latvian fisherfolk have lived here for centuries. Generation succeeded generation. Fair-haired lasses with coy glances and musical accents became in the course of time weather-beaten old women, wrapped in heavy shawls, and brawny youths in jaunty caps changed into imperturbable greybeards.

These fisherfolk go out to sea to catch sprats just as their forefathers did centuries ago, and, as centuries ago, some of them never return, particularly in the autumn, when violent gales rage in the Baltic, its icy waters foaming and frothing like a devil's cauldron. Over and over again heads are bared for those lost at sea. But never do the fishermen think of abandoning the occupation, perilous and hard, passed on to them by fathers and grandfathers. Undaunted, they face the dangers season after season.

Not far from the village a granite rock rises from the sea. It bears the inscription, carved by fishermen long years ago: "In memory of those lost and yet to be lost at sea."

When a Latvian writer told me of this inscription it seemed to me to be as sad as most epitaphs. But the Latvian shook his head.

"It is a very brave inscription," he said. "It testifies to indomitable spirit, be the dangers what they may. I would use it as the epigraph to any book extolling man's labour and perseverance. I would give it this interpretation: 'In memory of those who sailed and continue to sail the sea.' "

I agreed, and thought the epigraph, suitably adapted, could be used about writers and their work.

Not for a minute can the writer retreat before difficulties or obstacles. No matter what happens he must carry on where his predecessors left off and fulfil the mission entrusted to him by his contemporaries. How right Saltykov-Shchedrin was when he said that even a minute's silence on the part of literature would be equivalent to the death of the nation.

It is utterly wrong to regard writing merely as a craft or occupation. Writing is the expression of a noble inner urge to create.

And what is it that makes the writer follow that urge through torment and joy?

First of all—the imperative call of his own heart.

The voice of conscience and faith in the future do not permit one who feels in himself the urge to write to lead a barren existence and not convey the multifarious thoughts and emotions with which his soul is overflowing.

Yet it needs more than the call of the heart to make a writer of a man. Mostly in our youth when the fresh world of our emotions has neither been tempered nor battered by life, we writers echo the call of our own hearts. In our mature years we heed a more emphatic call, the call of the times, of our people, of humanity. We long to contribute to the sharpness of man's vision.

A man will go through hell's fire, will perform miracles to follow his inner urge.

A striking example in this respect is the life of Edward Dekker, the Dutch writer, better known under the penname of Multatuli, which in Latin means "long-suffering."

Unfortunately the best of his writings have not come down to us. This is the saddest part of the story I wish to tell about him.

My thoughts turned to Dekker in the little cottage on the Baltic dunes—perhaps because the same bleak sea washes the Netherlands, his own land. Of that land he had said with bitterness and shame: "I am son of the Netherlands, son of a land of robbers, lying between Friesland and Scheldt."

Dekker was wrong, of course. There are civilized robbers in Holland, but they are a tiny minority and by no means typical of the Dutch people. We all know Holland as a land of hard-working people with the spirit of the rebel Claas and Thyl Uylenspiegel. The spirit of Claas lives in the hearts of many Dutchmen, just as it lived in the heart of Multatuli.

Multatuli came of patrician stock. As a young man he graduated the university with honours and soon received a government appointment in Java. Later, he became governor of one of the island's provinces. Renown, favour, riches—all awaited him, even possibly, the post of viceroy. But the rebel spirit of Claas burned in Multatuli who scorned worldly wealth.

With rare courage and persistence he fought to put an end to the age-old subjugation of the Javanese by the Dutch. He always sided with the down-trodden natives and sought to redress their grievances. Under him all bribery was severely punished. When the people of Java rose against their oppressors, Multatuli, the highly placed Dutch government official, deeply sympathized with "these trusting children," as he called the Javanese. He condemned his fellow-countrymen for their harsh and unjust policy.

He denounced the stratagem to which the Dutch generals had resorted. The latter decided to take advantage of the Javanese weakness for cleanliness; cleanliness is inherent in the Javanese who abhor all filth. Knowing this, the generals ordered their soldiers to assault the natives with human excrement. And the Javanese who had

28

unflinchingly faced heavy artillery, quailed before this new trick and retreated.

Multatuli was not afraid to show his disdain for the Dutch generals and for the viceroy and his retinue—all self-professed Christians, of course. But what had they in common with the Christian maxim "Love thy neighbour as thyself"? His logic was unanswerable, but he could be put out of the way.

He was, of course, removed from his post and ordered home. As a member of the Dutch parliament for many years he pleaded for fair treatment for the Javanese, losing no opportunity to press his case, and sending petition after petition to the King and his ministers. But in vain! Nobody listened to him. They said he was a crank, even mad. His family went hungry.

It was then that he was seized by the urge to write. The urge evidently had been there all the time but now he felt a crying need to give it utterance. Multatuli wrote *Max Havelaar*, a scathing novel about the Dutch in Java. In this first attempt at fiction he was only feeling his way as a writer. But the book that followed, *Love Letters*, was written with amazing power, the power of one who had the courage of his convictions. In several chapters of this book he raises his voice in protest against the monstrous injustice that goes on in the world. In others he is caustic and witty in the pamphleteer manner. The last chapters are written with a touch of melancholy humour and are an attempt to revive that eager faith in humanity which is characteristic of childhood and youth.

"There can be no God, for God must be kind and good," writes Multatuli, and further: "When, alas, will they stop robbing the poor!"

Multatuli left Holland to look for earnings in other lands. His wife and children remained in Amsterdam—there was no money to pay for their fare.

Wrestling with poverty in the towns of Europe, Multatuli kept at his writing all the time—a mocking, tormented spirit, shunned by respectable society. Letters from home were few and far between. His poor wife was unable to spare the money for stamps. But he never ceased thinking of her and the children, especially of his youngest son; he feared that this little blue-eyed boy would lose his trust in people early in life and implored those at home to shelter him from needless disappointments.

Multatuli could find no publisher for his books.

But then the tide in his affairs unexpectedly turned. Some prominent Dutch publishers agreed to buy Multatuli's manuscripts on the condition that he relinquishes all publishing rights in their favour. Worn out by long struggling, Multatuli agreed. He returned to his native country. The publishers even advanced him a little money. But his books never saw light. Thus the offer to publish his works was merely a trick on the part of those in power to curb this staunch rebel whose pen made both the Dutch merchants and the government officials tremble for their safety.

Multatuli died with grim injustice staring him in the face. He died prematurely, died when so many more splendid books could have flowed from his pen, books written with the heart's blood.

Multatuli fought and perished in the struggle. He never flinched, but fought courageously, combining the life of militant politician and militant writer. Perhaps in the near future a monument will be erected to this great and unselfish man in Djokjakarta, capital of independent Java.

In passionate devotion to a purpose Multatuli had an equal in the painter Vincent van Gogh, also a Dutchman and his contemporary.

It is hard to find an example of greater self-abnegation in the name of art than is the life of Vincent van Gogh, who dreamed of setting up in France a sort of painters' community, the members of which could devote themselves wholly to their art.

How greatly van Gogh had suffered is well known. In his *Potato Eaters* and *Prisoners Walk* he shows the very depths of human despair. Yet it was not suffering he wished to portray but the joy of life.

Van Gogh's heart went out in sympathy for his fellow-creatures. It was to give them joy that he used to the full his extraordinary gift—the gift of seeing the world bathed in a wealth of colour and hues.

He longed to fill his canvases with joy. He painted his landscapes so that they seemed dipped in some miraculous fluid. There was such brilliance and solidity to his colours that every gnarled tree was like a sculpture and every clover field a warm stream of sunlight. He was a painter who used to the greatest possible effect every tint of colour, every hue.

He was poor, proud and impractical. He shared every bit of bread he had with the homeless and knew only too well from his own experience what social injustice was. He scorned cheap glory.

He was not a fighter—not one by nature. But he possessed heroism, the heroism of one who had a fanatical faith in a bright future for all men, for tillers of the soil, for miners, poets and scholars. But he was eager to say something to the world and he said it in the pictures he painted. Like all artists he expressed beauty. He chose to do it through the medium of colour. He was always deeply fascinated by Nature's wonderful colour combinations, showing how Nature's colours were ever changing, yet ever beautiful in every season and in every corner of the earth.

We must reconsider our appraisal of such painters as Vincent van Gogh, Vrubel, Borisov-Musatov, Gaugen and many others. The people of socialist society are heirs to all the spiritual riches of the world. We must banish from our midst the phillistine and the hypocrite who rant against beauty which exists despite their efforts to crush it.

From discussing literature I have wandered into the realm of painting. I have done this because acquaintance with all arts helps the writer to achieve perfection in his own field. But that is something I shall deal with later.

The sense that his vocation is one of the noblest there is must ever be present with the writer. A sober outlook and literary experience are nothing as compared with it. But the writer must not indulge in false heroics, nor in self-exaltation. He must not have an exaggerated notion of his role in society—nor of any of the qualities sometimes attributed to him as to a "being apart."

Mikhail Prishvin, a writer well aware of the high mission of literature, one who has indeed given his whole life to writing, said: "A writer is happy to regard himself not as one who stands apart from his fellow-men, but as one of the same flesh as they."

ARTIFICIAL FLOWERS

ften when my thoughts turn to creative writing I ask myself: "How and when does the urge to write originate? What first makes the writer pick up his pen and not put it down to the end of his days?"

It is hardest of all to recall when the urge to write first comes. I imagine that writing begins as a state of mind and that the urge to write is there long before one covers reams of paper with writing. To trace it to its source, perhaps, one should go back to one's childhood.

The world as we see it in our childhood is quite different from that of our mature years. Can one deny that the sun is most brilliant, the grass greenest, the sky bluest and each man a most marvellous being in our childhood? Each man is moreover a mysterious being—whether it is the carpenter with his clever tools and his smell of raw shavings or a scholar ready to explain why grass is green.

From our childhood we inherit the great gift of being fascinated by the world around us. He who retains this gift in later life is sure to become a poet or a writer, the difference between the two in the final analysis being not so great. Always to be finding novelty in everything is splendid soil for art to thrive and mature.

When I was at school I wrote poetry, like most boys, I suppose. And I wrote so much of it that at the end of each month I filled a thick note-book with my verses. The verses were bad; they were pretentious, ornate and "pretty." I can't even remember any of them now except for a line here and there, as for example:

Oh gather the flowers on stems drooping meekly!
In the fields rain is pattering bleakly,
And the winds to the sunset the dead leaves are
blowing,
Dusky-red in the autumn skies glowing ...

The more I wrote in my early youth, the more flowery my language grew. Often the lines were quite senseless.

For Saadi, the loved, sorrow glistens with opals,
On the pages of wearisome days...

For example, why sorrow should "glisten with opals" I cannot explain to this day. Most of the time I was, of course, merely carried away by the sound combinations of words and concerned myself not at all with the meaning.

It is interesting that many of my early poems were about the sea, of which in those days I had a very vague conception. I had in mind no definite sea; it was neither the Black, the Baltic, nor the Mediterranean Sea I devoted my poems to, but the sea of my imagination. I saw it as a glittering patchwork of colour, a great overstatement of everything I felt. Time and geographical entities had no place in what I wrote. To me the entire globe was then wrapped in romance as by thick layers of atmosphere. But the sea was the queen of romance—the foamy, rippling sea—home of winged vessels and sea-farers bold, its ports teeming with carefree throngs, and moving among them olive-skinned ladies of exquisite beauty caught in whirlpools of passion. That was how I thought of the sea in the romantic years of my youth.

As I grew older my verse became less ornamental and gradually less romantic. But, to tell the truth, I've never regretted the hold romance had over me in my youth. That is the time when romance is in our bones. Everything stirs our imagination, from the exotic beauty of the trop-ics to the glory of Civil War battles. Romance gives life that uncommon glow which is meat and drink to every young and imaginative creature. It is good to re-member Diderot's words about art: Art is that which finds the uncommon in the commonplace and the com-monplace in the uncommon.

In his imagination every youngster sees himself besieg-ing ancient castles, fighting for his life on a sinking vessel with its sails torn to shreds in the Strait of Magellan or near Novaya Zemlya, speeding down the steppes beyond the Ural Mountains in a machine-gun cart by the side of Chapayev, seeking the treasure hidden away by Stevenson on his mysterious island, hearing the flut-ter of the standards in the Battle of Borodino, or helping Mowgli in the trackless jungles of India.

Whenever I stay in the country (which is quite often) I take delight in watching the village children play their games. And what I notice is that they are always going on long sea voyages on rafts (in the village there is a shal-low lake), taking flights to the stars, or discovering new lands. Once I remember some of the neighbouring chil-dren having discovered a "new land" in the meadows and giving it a very romantic name. What they had actually come upon was an out-of-the-way lake with so many little creeks, and so overgrown with bulrush and reeds that it resembled a patch of elevated country.

I did not shed the romance of my youth all at once. It lingered in my heart like the fragrance of lilacs in summer. It lent a glow to Kiev, a city I knew so well that I was even getting a little weary of it. It made me admire the golden sunsets that blazed in its gardens. Beyond the Dnieper I watched the lightning streak its dark skies and saw there in my mind's eye a land, stormy and sultry, filled with the ripply rustling of leaves. In spring the chestnut trees dropped their creamy blossoms with red-dotted petals upon the city. And there were so many of these blossoms that when it rained they checked the flow of the water, virtually turning some of the streets into small lakes. After rain the blue bowl of Kiev's sky gleamed with the colour of moonstone. And then the following lines came back to me with unexpected force:

> *Spring's magic reigns, with sweet caress,*
> *With starlit skies unfurled,*
> *You brought me word of happiness*
> *In this, our futile world. . .*

It was at this time that I first began to think of love. I was at the age when all girls seemed beautiful to me. I was conscious of their presence everywhere, in the streets, in the gardens, in the trams. A coy glance in my direction, a whiff of fragrance from girlish locks, a row of gleaming teeth revealed through half-open lips, the glimpse of a delicately moulded knee under wind-blown skirts, a touch of cool fingers—all stirred me deeply, filling me with mysterious longings, and I knew that sooner or later love would come my way.

The writing of verses and these vague longings filled the greater part of my youth, which was by no means happy.

Soon I gave up writing verses because I realized that I had been producing rubbish—pretty artificial flowers with a saccharine sweetness.

I turned to short story writing. My first attempt in this field has a history of its own.

MY FIRST SHORT STORY

rom the little town of Chernobyl I planned to go by boat along the Pripyat to Kiev. I had spent the summer in Chernobyl on the estate of Levkovich, a retired general. I was recommended to him by my schoolmaster as a coach for one of his sons, a lazy, stupid boy who had failed in two examinations.

The old manor-house was situated in a dip in the country with a cold mist drifting over it in the evening, frogs croaking loudly in the neighbouring swamps and the marsh tea plant smelling strong enough to cause a headache. At tea-time the general's madcap boys shot wild ducks from the terrace.

General Levkovich was a heavily built man with a grey moustache and black bulging eyes. Irascible and afflicted with asthma, he sat all day long in an armchair on the terrace, wheezing and now and then shouting hoarsely: "Do you call this a family, this pack of good-for-nothings? They've turned the house into a pigsty. I'll drive every one of them out and won't leave them a penny."

But no one paid the slightest attention to him. For it was Madame Levkovich, his well-preserved, coquettish, thrifty wife, who walked about all the summer in a tightly laced, squeaky corset, that ran the household and the estate.

Besides his good-for-nothing sons, the general had a daughter, a girl of twenty, nicknamed Joan of Arc. This young girl spent most of the day galloping on a fierce bay stallion. She rode astride like a man and pretended to be a *femme fatale*. "Despicable" was a pet word of hers which she repeated endlessly.

When I was introduced to her she held out her hand from the saddle of her horse and, staring me in the face, said: "Despicable!"

All the time I was there I kept thinking of how to make my escape from this crazy family and was intensely relieved when I at last found myself seated on some hay covered with a cloth in the dogcart which was to take me off to my boat. The driver, Ignatius Loyola (everybody had a nickname, the name of some historical personage, in the Levkovich household), or for short Ignat, tugged at the reins and we set off at a trot to Chernobyl, the thickets beyond the gates greeting us with silence.

We arrived in Chernobyl at sunset only to discover that my boat was late and that we would have to spend the night at the inn.

The innkeeper, an elderly Jew called Koosher, put me up in a small room hung with the pictures of his ancestors—grey-bearded old men in silk skull-caps, and be-wigged old ladies wrapped in black lace shawls. All the old ladies had tearful eyes.

A stench of kerosene came from the kitchen lamp. No sooner had I climbed atop the high feather-bed than an army of bedbugs made for me from all the chinks and cracks in the walls. I sprang out of bed, dressed hurriedly, and went out on the porch.

In front of me stretched the Pripyat, shimmering with a dull gleam. Logs were piled up on its bank. I sat down on a bench and put up my coat-collar. It was a cold night and I shivered. On the porch steps sat two men dimly visible in the dark. One was smoking shag, the other, crouching, seemed to doze. From the yard came the driver's loud snoring; he had gone to sleep on the hay in the cart and now I envied him.

"Bedbugs?" said the man who was smoking in a high-pitched voice.

I recognized him by his voice as the short, glum-looking Jew, with bare feet stuck in galoshes, who, as we drew up at the inn, had opened the gates for us and demanded ten kopeks for this service. I had given him the coin. Koosher, who caught sight of him from the window of the inn, had shouted. "Get out of my yard, you beggar, I've told you that a thousand times." The Jew had not even as much as glanced at Koosher. "Did you hear that?" he said to me with a wink. "Each ten-kopek piece he touches burns his hand. The man's so greedy, he'll die of it, mark my words!"

I asked Koosher who the wretch was. "Oh, that's Joseph, the mad one," he replied reluctantly. "Begs for a living yet has no respect for anyone, looks on you like he were King David sitting on his throne."

"I bet Koosher'll charge you extra for the bedbugs," said Joseph to me, and I saw that his chin had several days' stubble on it. "Once a man's got it into his head to make a fortune nothing's too dirty for him."

"Joseph!" the crouching man beside him cut in suddenly in a testy voice. "Why did you kill my Christina? Can't find peace because of it now for two years."

"Oh, Nikifor, only a man without a grain of sense can say such filthy words," Joseph cried resentfully. "I killed her, you say! Go to your Father Mikhail and ask *him* who killed her. Or to the police officer Sukharenko."

"My only daughter!" Nikifor cried in dismay. "There is no sun shining for me now, it's gone behind the bogs for ever and ever."

"Oh, shut up, will you?"

"They won't even let me mourn her like a Christian," Nikifor went on, paying no attention to Joseph. "Tell you what I'll do, I'll go to Kiev to the Metropolitan, won't leave him alone till he washes away her sins."

"Shut up!" repeated Joseph. "For one hair of her head I'd give my whole rotten life. And you say. . . ."

Then he suddenly broke down, the sobs sticking in his throat. In an effort to control them, he let out a feeble wail.

"So, you're whining, you fool, good!" said Nikifor composedly and even approvingly. "If Christina hadn't loved you, you miserable rascal, I'd have made short work of you and it'd be no sin."

"Go ahead, make short work of me!" cried Joseph. "Maybe that's just what I'm hankering after. It'd be better for me to rot in the grave than. . . ."

"You were a fool and you still are one," Nikifor retorted sadly. "But I'll do it when I come back from Kiev, so you'll stop wringing my heart. It's all too much for my poor heart, I tell you."

"And who'll watch your shack when you go?" asked Joseph, now his old self again.

"Nobody. Boarded it up. What do I want with a shack now? Do the dead need a place to live?"

While I was listening to this strange conversation, a thick mist gathered over the river. From the damp logs on the shore came a pungent odour like that of medicine and the silence was broken by the lazy barking of dogs.

"If only we knew when the damn boat is going to

come," said Nikifor vexedly. "We could go and get ourselves some drinks, Joseph, just to make things a little easier. But where's one to get drinks this time of night?"

I felt warmer now and leaning against the wall began to doze.

In the morning there was still no boat. Koosher said it must have anchored for the night somewhere because of the fog and that when it arrived it would stay for a few hours in Chernobyl. I had my tea. Ignatius Loyola, the driver, drove back to the estate.

To kill time I set out for the town. Down the main street several shops were open, smelling of herring and laundry soap. A crooked sign on one of the doors proclaimed a barber shop. In the doorway stood its freckled proprietor chewing sunflower seeds. Having nothing better to do I stepped in for a shave. Sighing, the barber lathered my chin and began to question me politely— the usual questions they ask in provincial places—as to who I was, and what had brought me to the town.

Suddenly a group of boys whisked past the barber shop whistling and making faces, and then came Joseph's voice singing:

> *My song shall ne'er wake*
> *My beauty from her sleep . . .*

"Lazar," came a woman's voice from behind the timber partition, "bolt the door. Joseph's drunk again. My God, what's going to happen next?"

The barber bolted the door and drew the curtain.

"As soon as he sees a customer in the shop, he's sure to dash in and begin to sing, dance and bawl," explained the barber.

"What's the matter with him?" I asked.

Before he could reply, a young and dishevelled wom-

42

an, her eyes startlingly bright with excitement, appeared from behind the partition.

"Listen to me, customer," she began, "firstly, let me say 'how d'ye do?' secondly, Lazar'll never know how to tell the story, because, well—can men understand a woman's heart, I ask you? What?! Don't you wag your silly head, Lazar! Let me tell him the story and give him something to think about. Let the gentleman know what a young girl will do for the sake of love."

"Manya," said the barber, "calm yourself!"

Joseph's voice could be heard from afar:

Come to my grave when I may die
With a bottle of home-brew and some sausage pie.

"My, it's awful!" the woman cried. "And to think it's the same Joseph who was going to qualify for a doctor's assistant at Kiev, son of Pesya, the kindest soul in Chernobyl. Thank God she hasn't lived to see him come to this. Can you imagine, customer, a woman loving a man so dearly that she is ready to bear any torture for his sake."

"There you're off again, Manya," exclaimed the barber, "I'm sure the gentleman doesn't understand a thing you're saying."

"All right, I'll begin with the town fair," said Manya. "And who should come to this fair, but Nikifor, a widowed forester from Karpilovka way, with his only daughter Christina. Now there was a girl, I tell you! If you'd seen her you'd be ready to die for her. Her eyes—I tell you they were as blue as that bit of sky over there, and her braids as fair as though she'd dipped them in gold. And she was so sweet, and slender! Joseph as soon as he sat eyes on her lost his power of speech. He fell in love at first sight. But that, of course, is not to be wondered at. The tsar himself, if he had set eyes on her, would be pining away for her right now. What is to be wondered at is that the girl fell in love with him. You've seen Joseph? A shrimp, a red-head and with the funniest ways. Well, to make a long story short, Christina left her father's home and went to live with Joseph. You should see Joseph's place. It'd make you sick. A goat would feel cramped there, let alone three grown-ups. But, when all is said and done, it was a clean place. And what do you think Pesya did? Welcomed the girl like she was a princess. And Christina and Joseph began to live well— like man and wife. Joseph was in heaven, of course. But do you know what it means for a Jew to love a gentile? They can never be wedded. And then, of course, the whole town was set a-cackling like a regiment of hens. Joseph decided to take the Christian faith and went to Father Mikhail. 'You should have thought of conversion before you deflowered a Christian maid,' the priest told him. 'You acted contrariwise, and now I won't baptize you without the Metropolitan's own consent.' Whereupon Joseph called him a dirty name and left. Then it was that our rabbi interfered. He found out that Joseph wanted to turn Christian and he cursed him and his at the synagogue down to the tenth generation. And to cap it all, Nikifor came and on his knees begged Christina to go back with him. But she only shed tears and gave no answer. Then some dirty folk set the town's boys to teasing poor Christina. 'Say, kosher Christina,' they shouted at her, 'will you have some Christian meat?' And they made noses at her. In the streets the people stared after her and laughed. There were some who even threw dung at her from behind a fence. And they smeared Pesya's house with tar!"

"Ah, Pesya!" the barber exclaimed with a sigh. "What a woman!"

"Stop interrupting!" Manya shouted at him. "The rabbi called for Pesya and said: 'You breed sin in your home, my esteemed Pesya Izraelevna. You have trespassed the law. I can lay a curse on you and yours and Jehovah will punish you as he would a street woman. Have compassion on your own grey locks.' And what do you think she answered? 'You are no rabbi,' she said, 'you're worse than a policeman! Two young people love each other, and why should you butt into their affairs?' She spat and went out. The rabbi excommunicated her, too. They know how to muzzle folk out here. Only don't say I said so. The whole town buzzed with the affair. Then district policeman Sukharenko called for Joseph and Christina: 'As for you, Joseph, I'm locking you up in gaol for insulting Father Mikhail, a man of God,' he said. 'And I'll see you get a taste of the labour gangs yet. And you, Christina, have got to go home to your father. I give you three days to make up your mind. You two have stirred up the whole *uyezd*. I'll be getting into trouble from His Excellency, the Governor-General, before I know it.'

"And without further ado, Sukharenko thrust Joseph into a cell. He said afterwards he did it only to frighten him. And you won't believe what happened: Christina died of grief. To watch her after Joseph was imprisoned made kind folks' hearts go out in pity for her. She wept for several days until she had no more tears. Her eyes dried up and she would have nothing to eat, begging only that they let her see Joseph. On Yom Kippur, the Day of Atonement, she went to sleep never to rise again. She lay white and happy as though thankful to God for having taken her away from such a rotten life. Why had she been so punished as to fall in love with Joseph, I ask you, why? Surely there are plenty of other men in the world. Sukharenko let Joseph out, but from that day he's been stark mad, and has taken to drinking and begging."

"I would have preferred death in his place," said the barber. "Would have shot myself through the head."

"You men think you are so very brave!" Manya cried contemptuously. "But when it comes down to brass tacks you'll run a mile a minute from death. When love scorches a woman's heart it's a different matter. That you can't understand!"

"It's all the same, I tell you, whether it's a man's heart or a woman's!" replied the barber, shrugging.

From the barber's I went directly to the inn. Neither Joseph nor Nikifor was there. Koosher I found sitting drinking tea at the window in a vest that had seen better days with fat flies buzzing about him.

It was not till the evening that the boat arrived, and it lay at Chernobyl till late at night. A worn oilskin couch in the salon served as my berth. At night the fog had gathered again, and the boat tied up to the shore. I did not find Nikifor on board, so he must have gone and got drunk with Joseph.

I have dwelt in such detail on this story because of the effect it had on me. As soon as I returned to Kiev I threw my note-books with all my verses into the fire. Without a pang of regret I watched the sheets with their fancy phrases about "foamy crystals" and "sapphire skies" curl into ashes.

The story I had heard had a good sobering effect on me. I realized what rubbish I had been writing about love, comparing it with the "languor of dying lilies," while here lumps of dung were cast at a beautiful woman who loved.

These thoughts brought back to me words I once heard: "A horrid age breeds horrid hearts." I decided to write my first short story—about Christina. "A true story," I said to myself.

I worked at it for a long time, but could not understand why it was coming out so colourless and insipid despite its dramatic intensity. Then it dawned upon me: in the first place, there was the difficulty of writing a story from another's words; in the second place, I had made the mistake of becoming wholly absorbed in Christina's love and giving too little attention to the savage "small town" morality of which she was a victim.

I rewrote the story, somewhat surprised that in doing so no refined or beautiful words came to my mind. The story required hard truth and simplicity.

When it was finished I took it to the editor of a magazine which had previously published some of my verses.

"A waste of time," said the editor. "Can't print such stuff. Why, for that description of the police officer alone we'd get into trouble. But there's guts in the story. Bring us something else—and you'd better use a pen-name if you don't want to get kicked out of school."

I took the story back and put it away. When, the following spring I happened to reread it I understood yet another thing: I had not put enough of myself into the story—my indignation, my thoughts, my admiration for Christina's love. I rewrote the story once again and took it to the editor—this time not to have it published but for an opinion. The editor read it through in my presence, and slapping me on the back said: "Good stuff!"

I realized then that a writer must express what is in his mind and heart fully and unreservedly even in a short story like this, thus voicing the spirit of his times and the aspirations of his own people. There must be no shame in revealing anything before the reader, no fear in repeating what has already been said by other writers (though, of course, through the prism of one's own thoughts and feelings); no thought of what the critics or editors would say.

The writer gives himself wholly to what he is writing, forgetting everything else, and he writes as though he is writing to himself or to the being dearest to him in the whole world. Only then can he give full rein to his thoughts and let them flow freely. And he will find to his amazement that there are far more thoughts, more feeling and poetic power in him than he had ever supposed there to be. Thus the creative process is set in motion, and as it runs its course it acquires new qualities, becomes more complex and richer.

The creative process may be likened to spring. The sun's rays melt the snow, warm the air, the soil and the trees. They fill the earth with a humming and a rippling, with the play of drops and running water—the thousand signs of spring. Likewise, the creative process, once begun, calls forth a constant flow of fresh thoughts and images, sensations and words, so that the writer himself is sometimes astounded at the result.

One can become a writer only when one has something new, significant and interesting to say and when one can see a good deal which escapes the notice of others.

To return to myself, I must say that when I first began to write I realized only too poignantly that I had very little to say, and also that the impulse to create, if it is not fed, can be as easily extinguished as it is kindled. My store of life's observations was infinitesimal. Book knowledge outweighed my knowledge of life. I felt this keenly and knew that I must fill myself with life to the very brim.

To do this I dropped writing completely—for ten years. And as Maxim Gorky had said I went "out into the world." I began to tramp the country, trying my hand at various jobs and knocking about with all sorts of people. I did not go out of my way "to observe life" or "collect facts" for future books. I lived as all people do, working, loving, suffering, hoping, dreaming. Yet, for all that, at the back of my mind, there was the ever-present thought that some day, sooner or later, perhaps even in my old age, I would begin to write—not because it was my ambition to become a writer, but because my whole being cried out for it and because literature to me was the most wonderful thing in the world.

LIGHTNING

ow does the writer get an idea for his book or story? Since there are hardly two ideas which arise and develop in the writer's mind in the same way, the answer to this question will be different in each case.

It is easier to answer the question: what precedes the birth of an idea for a literary work? The answer is—the writer's mental state.

Perhaps I can best explain what I mean by drawing a comparison. Comparisons to my mind often help to shed light on a complicated problem. The astronomer James Jeans, for example, when asked what he thought was the age of the earth, replied: "Imagine," he said, "a gigantic mountain, say Mt. Elbrus in the Caucasus, and think of a little sparrow pecking away light-heartedly at it. Well then, the earth has been in existence as many years as it would take that sparrow to peck the mountain to its very base."

I'll draw a much simpler comparison to show how an idea is conceived in the writer's mind. Let us compare the idea itself to a flash of lightning. It takes many days for electricity to accumulate over the earth. But when a very great amount of it has accumulated, the atmosphere becomes so overcharged with it that the white cumuli are turned into dark thunder clouds and the electric charges burst into a spark. Thus lightning appears. And it is almost immediately followed by torrents of rain.

In very much the same way an idea for a story or novel flashes across the writer's consciousness when it is brimming over with thoughts, emotions and memories, accumulated gradually, little by little, until they have reached a point of saturation and demand an outlet. And it is in an idea for a new story or novel that this crammed and somewhat chaotic world of thought and emotion finds an outlet.

It often needs but some slight stimulus for the idea to arise. It may be a chance meeting with somebody, a word, casual, but full of meaning, a dream, the sound of a far-off voice, the sunlight playing in a drop of water, a steamer's whistle. Anything in the world around us and in our own selves can be that stimulus.

Lev Tolstoi saw a broken burdock and it gave him the idea for his splendid story *Khadzhi-Murat*, the idea coming like a flash of lightning. On the other hand if Tolstoi had not lived in the Caucasus and had not heard there about Khadzhi-Murat, the burdock, of course, would not have started the train of thought that gave him the idea for the story. Tolstoi's inner consciousness was prepared for the subject and the burdock was merely instrumental in igniting it.

The idea when it first occurs to the writer is often very vague. "Dimly as yet I discerned the illusive outlines of my novel in the magic crystal of my mind," Pushkin wrote. Gradually it takes shape, possesses the brain and heart of the writer who turns it over and over in his mind.

The process of thought crystallization and enrichment goes on every hour and every day of the writer's life. It goes on in the most natural way, affected by the writer's daily experiences, his sorrows and joys, and in the closest contact with reality. For the writer must never stand aloof from life, never shrink into himself. Nothing will help the development of his idea better than contact with life.

There are many wrong and trite notions current about literary creation, particularly about inspiration—so trite as to be quite repugnant. There is, for example, *The Poet and the Tsar*, a film about Pushkin which many still remember. Pushkin is shown sitting with raised eyes, then convulsively seizing his quill-pen, he begins to write, stops, rolls his eyes upwards, chews at his pen, and hurriedly jots down some lines. These actions were evidently copied from the many paintings in which the Russian poet is depicted as an ecstatic madman.

And when inspiration visits a composer (and it must do no other thing but "visit" him), he must stand, it seems, with uplifted gaze conducting for himself the entrancing music that doubtlessly at the moment rings in his soul. This is how Chaikovsky is depicted on the sugar-sweet monument of him in Moscow.

If inspiration is to be defined at all, it is to be defined as a working condition that has nothing to do with a theatrical pose.

Pushkin in his accurate and simple way spoke thus of inspiration: "Inspiration is the vigorous receptivity of the soul, its quick grasp of things paving the way for their explanation. Critics," he said further, "confuse inspiration with exultation." In the same way readers sometimes confuse verisimilitude with truth.

That is not so terrible. But when there are painters and sculptors who confound inspiration with some foolish ecstasy it is a sign of utter ignorance and inconsideration of the hard toil of the writer.

According to Chaikovsky, inspiration is no flourish of the baton but a state when one works to the uttermost, with heart and soul. I beg to be excused for this digression. But all that I have said above is not unimportant for it shows that the Philistine is still among us.

Everyone has at least a few times in his life experienced a state of inspiration—an elevation of the soul, a fresh perception of reality, a flood of thoughts and a consciousness of one's creative powers.

Inspiration is a working condition with a romantic undertone, a between-the-lines poetic commentary.

Inspiration comes to us like a sunny summer morning which had cast off the mists of a quiet night. It breathes tenderly into our face a cool, restorative breath.

Inspiration is like first love when the heart beats loudly in anticipation of joyful meetings, of loving looks and smiles and words unsaid. Delicately and unerringly our mental state is tuned like some magic musical instrument and it echoes even the most deeply hidden sounds of life.

Many writers and poets have said beautiful things about inspiration. "Let but the divine word touch our tender ear," wrote Pushkin. "The sound approaches and hearkening to it my soul grows young," said Blok. To Lermontov, inspiration was "an assuaging of the soul." The poet Fet is extremely accurate in defining inspiration:

> With but one turn to steer the vessel's helm
> Away from shores where tides have smoothed the
> sands,
> To ride upon the wave into another realm,
> To scent the breezes from the flowering lands.
> With but one word to rend the calm despondent,
> Be overwhelmed with something dear, unknown,
> To be released, pour balm on secret torments,
> To feel another's instantly your own...

Turgenev called inspiration the "approach of God," a luminescence of thought and emotion. And he shuddered when he spoke of the torments which the writer goes through to put these thoughts and emotions into words.

Tolstoi's definition of inspiration was very simple. "Inspiration," he said, "is that which suddenly reveals what one is capable of accomplishing. The stronger the inspiration, the greater pains must be taken to bring it to fulfilment."

But whatever we may say about inspiration it is never sterile, it feeds the urge to create. It bears fruit.

CHARACTERS REVOLT

Long before the Revolution when people moved from one flat to another they sometimes hired convicts from the local gaol to help with the furniture.

Naturally we children were curious to see the convicts whom we pitied greatly.

They usually arrived escorted by mustachioed warders with huge pistols tucked in their belts. They wore faded grey convict suits and brimless grey caps. Some were in irons fastened with straps to their belts and for these for some reason we had the highest regard. The convicts' presence gave the place an air of mystery. But we youngsters were not a little surprised to find that most of these unfortunates were no different from other human beings, except for their emaciated look, and some were so good-natured that it was impossible to associate them with villainy or crime. They were politeness itself and when moving the furniture were in deadly terror of knocking against somebody or breaking something.

Eager to do them a kindness, with our parents' support, we resorted to a little stratagem. We would beg

Mother to take the prison guards into the kitchen and treat them to tea. When they were out of the way we would hurriedly stuff the convicts' pockets with bread, sausage, sugar, tobacco and sometimes money given to us by our elders. Imagining ourselves party to a great conspiracy, we were delighted to hear the convicts thank us in undertones, wink in the direction of the kitchen, and replace our presents in secret inside pockets.

Sometimes the convicts would furtively pass letters on to us to be posted. We would glue stamps on them and then all in a bunch pretending we were conspirators go very secretively to mail them, looking around to see that there were no "coppers" nearby as though the latter could possibly guess whose letters we were posting.

I remember one of the convicts particularly well to this day. He was a grey-bearded old fellow, evidently a gang leader. He supervised the moving of the furniture. Now the furniture, particularly large cupboards and pianos, had a way of getting stuck in doorways, or slipping out of the convicts' hands at the wrong moment. It was often quite useless to try to squeeze some piece into the new place assigned for it.

"Put the thing wherever it means to stand," the leader would order in such cases. "I've been working with furniture now for the last five years and I'm up to its tricky ways. I tell you if a thing doesn't want to stand where you're putting it, it won't and that's all. It'll break but have its way."

It was in connection with writers' outlines and characters that I remembered this old convict's bit of wisdom. The characters in a book, just like the furniture, want to have their own way. They will take up the cudgels with the author and as often as not emerge victorious.

Most writers draw up an outline for whatever they intend to write. Some work out very detailed plans, others very tentative ones. Still others jot down seemingly unconnected words.

Only writers with a born gift for improvisation are able to sit down and write without some sort of a plan. Among Russian writers Pushkin possessed this gift to a great degree, and among our contemporary writers Alexei Tolstoi.

Allowances should be made for the geniuses of literature. These may have followed no plan. Possessing very rich natures, any subject, thought, incident or object could set them off on a ceaseless train of associations.

"See that ash-tray on your table," said young Chekhov to the writer Korolenko one day. "Would you like me to sit down and write a story about it?" and Chekhov, of course, would have been as good as his word.

A writer may see or picture a man picking up a crumpled ruble from the pavement. That gives him the idea for the beginning of a novel and he begins it in an offhand manner. It runs smoothly and facilely. And soon the chapters he writes expand in depth and breadth, become filled with people, events, with light and colour and flow freely and powerfully, the stream of action spurred by the writer's imagination and drawing from his precious store of image and language. The narrative set rolling by a slight incident which fired the writer's imagination develops in content and complexity of character. The writer is in the power of his own thoughts and emotions, ready to weep over his manuscript like Dickens, or groan with pain like Flaubert, or roar with laughter like Gogol.

In the same way some distant sound such as the far-away report of a hunter's gun in the hills starts the movement of gleaming sheets of snow down over the steep mountain slopes. Soon they are sweeping down in an avalanche into the valley below, shaking the earth around and filling the air with glittering whiteness.

Much has been written about the facility with which the greatest among the great, particularly those possessing the gift of improvisation, have been able to create. Baratinsky, who frequently watched Pushkin at work, wrote: "Young Pushkin, that brilliant, light-hearted creature—with what ease his vigorous verse flowed from his pen. . . ."

I have already said that some writers' plans for their books seem to be a jumble of words and nothing else. This is true of my own plan for my short story called "Snow." Before I began to write it I made some desultory notes which filled a sheet of foolscap. Here is what I wrote:

"A forgotten book about the North. The colour of foil predominates in the northern landscape. A steaming river—women rinsing clothes in the ice-holes. Smoke. Tablet over Alexandra Ivanovna's door-bell with two inscriptions. War. Tanya. Where can she be? Living in some remote place? Alone? A wan moon in the clouds—far, far away. Life caught in a small circle of lamplight. All night there is a creaking in the walls. Tree branches rapping on the window-panes. We rarely go out in the dark winter nights. That's something to be verified. Solitude and expectation. An old, grumpy cat that won't be humoured. All things seem visible, even the olive-coloured candles over the grand piano. A woman singer looks for rooms with a piano. Evacuation. Expectation. A strange house. Old-fashioned, in its own way comfortable, with a stale tobacco smell. An old man had lived and died there. A walnut desk with yellow stains on the green cloth. A little girl—Cinderella. A nurse. Nobody else so far. Love, they say, attracts from a distance. Expectation—that's something one can write a whole story about. Waiting for what? For whom? She does not know herself. It is heart-breaking. People meet by chance at a cross-roads not knowing that all of their past life had been a preparation for their meeting. Theory of probability—as applied to human hearts. Fools find everything very simple. Snow, snow, endless snow. The man is destined to come. Letters addressed to the dead man keep arriving. They are piled up on the desk. The key is in these letters, in their nature and in their contents. The seaman. The son. Dread that he may arrive. Expectation. Her generosity knows no bounds. The letters become a reality. Again the candles. A change in the quality of things. Music notes. A towel with embroidered oak leaves. A grand piano. Smoke of burning birch. A tuner—all Czechs are splendid musicians. The mystery is cleared up!"

By some stretch of the imagination this may be considered as a plan for my story. Anyone looking through the notes without having read the story will yet realize that they represent a determined, though vague, groping for theme and plot.

However, generally the writer's most painstaking and thorough plans are the most short-lived; for no sooner do the characters of the story come on the scene, no sooner do they begin to live than they rise up in arms against the author. Thereupon the story begins to unfold in obedience to its own inner logic, the characters acting as their natures will it, though the writer, of course, is their creator.

If the writer insists on keeping the characters within the framework of his plan and preventing them from developing in their own way, the characters will cease to be people of flesh and blood and become mere cardboard figures.

When a visitor to Tolstoi's home in Yasnaya Polyana told the great writer that he had been cruel to make the lovely Anna Karenina throw herself under a moving train, he replied: "What you say reminds me of a story told about Pushkin. The poet once said to a friend of his: 'Just think what a trick Tatyana has played on me. She's gone and got married. Never expected it of her.' I can say the same about Anna Karenina. My characters sometimes do things I don't in the least want them to do. In fact they do the things that are done in life, and not what I intend them to do."

All writers know how intractable their characters can get. "Right in the middle of my writing I never know what my characters will do or say the next minute and I watch them with amazement," Alexei Tolstoi used to say.

Sometimes an insignificant character will supplant the more important ones and become the principal figure, forcing a change in the course of events.

It is while he is writing that a story really begins to live in the writer's imagination. Therefore if the outline goes to pieces it is no calamity. It is quite natural for it to be swept aside by life and for life to invade the writer's sheets of paper.

But that does not mean that writers' outlines are useless, that the writer's business is merely to set down on paper whatever comes into his head on the spur of the moment. When all is said and done, the life of the characters is after all conditioned by the writer's consciousness, by his imagination, his store of memories and his mental state.

THE STORY OF A NOVEL

LOOKING AT MARS

shall try to recall how I had got my idea for *Kara-Bogaz* and how I came to write this novel.

This takes me back to my childhood which I spent in Kiev. There overlooking the Dnieper was a little hill called Vladimirskaya Gorka. Every evening an elderly man in a queer old hat with drooping sides climbed to the top of this hill setting up an ancient telescope on a rickety iron tripod. The man was known round town as the "Astrologer" and considered to be an Italian. He deliberately spoke a broken Russian.

"Dear Signori and Signore, buon guorno," he would begin in a monotone after the telescope was set up. "For the price of five kopeks you can get a close view of the moon and the stars. I recommend you particularly to look at the ill-omened planet of Mars. It has the colour of human blood. He who is born under the star of Mars may yet meet his death from a bullet on the battlefield."

Once when I happened to be with Father on the hill I took a look at Mars through the telescope. I saw a black vacuum and in the midst of it a reddish ball. I watched the ball get nearer and nearer the edge of the telescope until it disappeared behind its copper rim. The "Astrologer" turned the telescope slightly and Mars was back in its old place but soon again began sliding towards the rim.

"Can you see anything?" asked my father.

"Certainly," I replied. "I can even see the canals the Martians built." I said this because I knew that the Martians had dug huge canals on the surface of their planet. Why they had done so I did not know.

"That's going a little too far," said Father. "The only astronomer who saw these canals was the Italian Schiaparelli, and he, of course, had a powerful telescope."

Father's mentioning Schiaparelli, presumably a fellow-countryman of the "Astrologer," produced no impression on the latter.

"I see another planet to the left of Mars," I said uncertainly. "And it's flitting in all directions."

"Ha, ha," laughed the "Astrologer" good-naturedly. "You've taken a beetle on the lens for a planet," he said, breaking unexpectedly into a strong Ukrainian accent and giving his real nationality away.

He took off his hat and waved away the beetle.

Looking at Mars gave me a feeling of cold and fright. It was a relief to get away from the telescope and walk on the solid earth of the Kiev streets which, with their dim lamplight, the rumbling wheels of carriages and the dusty scent of wafted chestnut blossoms, seemed particularly colourful, and dependable to me. I certainly had no wish to travel to the moon or to Mars.

"Why is Mars a red-brick colour?" I asked Father.

Father told me that Mars, which had once been very much like our own earth, with seas, mountains and luxuriant vegetation, was now a dying planet. Gradually the seas and rivers had dried up on it, the vegetation had disappeared and the mountains were levelled by the winds. Today it was nothing but a colossal, barren desert covered with reddish sands because the mountains on its surface had once been of red rock.

"Does that mean that Mars is a ball of sand?" I asked.

"Most likely," Father agreed. "What had happened to Mars," he added, "may happen to our own earth. Some day it too may be transformed into a desert. But it will take millions and millions of years to do that. So we needn't worry about it now. Besides by then man might have invented a means of averting such a calamity."

I assured Father I was not in the least worried or frightened. But to tell the truth I was both. To think only that such a misfortune could befall our planet. When I got home I learned from my elder brother that even to-day half of the earth's surface was desert.

From that time on a sort of desertphobia had got hold of me. I hated and feared the desert though I had never seen it; and all the stories I read about the Sahara, the simoons and camels, "ships of the desert," had no allurement for me.

Some time later when our family moved to the country to stay with my grandfather, Maxim Grigoryevich, I had my real first taste of the desert and it in no way allayed my fears.

It was a warm and rainy summer. The grass had grown tall and thick, the nettles at the wattle-fence reaching almost to man's height. Full-eared corn swayed in the fields. A pungent odour of fennel came from the vegetable gardens. Everything pointed to a good harvest.

But one day as I sat on the river-bank, angling for gudgeons, Grandfather, who was at my side, rose quickly to his feet and shading his eyes with his hand stared at the fields across the river.

"It's coming, the devil! May it perish for ever and ever!" he said and spat with vexation.

I looked in the same direction but saw nothing except a whirling dark wave rolling fast in our direction. I took it for the approach of a storm but Grandad said:

"It's a dry wind from the Bukhara desert. It'll bring a spell of heat that'll parch the land, a real calamity, son."

Meanwhile the ominous wave rolled right at us.

"Run home," Grandad said to me, hurriedly gathering up his fishing tackle, "or your eyes'll get full of dust. I'll come along, too, in a minute. Be quick!"

I ran to the cottage but the hot desert wind overtook me on the way. It came laden with sand, whirling and whistling, and sending flurries of birds' feathers and chips of wood into the air. A heavy haze obscured everything. The sun had suddenly grown shaggy and red as Mars. Broom-plants swayed and crackled. A heat wave scorched my back. It seemed to me that my shirt was smouldering. Dust crunched between my teeth and pricked my eyes.

My aunt Fedosya Maximovna was standing in the doorway of the cottage holding an icon wrapped in an embroidered cloth.

"Lord, have mercy on us!" she muttered with fright. "Blessed Virgin, save us!"

Just then the sand-storm swept upon the cottage causing the loose window-panes to rattle, and tousling the straw on the roof from which sparrows shot out like volleys of bullets.

Father was not with us. He had remained in Kiev. And Mother was terribly alarmed.

The growing heat was impossible to bear. It seemed that in no time the straw on the roof would catch fire and that our hair and clothes would begin to burn, too. I burst into tears. By evening the leaves on the dense shrubs had withered and hung in grey tatters. There were sand-drifts round the wattle-fences. And by morning the foliage was seared and shrivelled, the leaves so dry that they could easily be crushed to powder in the hand. The wind now blew even stronger, sweeping down the dead leaves, so that many of the trees stood as bare and black as in late autumn.

Grandfather had been to the fields. He returned perplexed and downcast, his hands trembling so that he couldn't undo the tassels at the collar of his homespun shirt.

"If it won't stop in the night," he said, "the corn is lost, and the orchards and vegetable gardens, too."

The wind did not abate. It blew for a fortnight, sometimes a little weaker, but only to start afresh with greater force, turning the land into a grey wilderness right before our eyes. Women's wailing filled the cottages. The men sat glumly in the shelter of the wall, prodding the soil with their sticks.

"It's turning hard as rock," they said. "The grip of death's on the land that's what it is, and people have nowhere to go."

Father came to take us back to Kiev. To my questions concerning the desert winds he replied reluctantly.

"Yes, the desert's spreading to the Ukraine," he said, "and that's the ruin of the crops."

"Can't something be done?" I asked.

"Not a thing, unless we erect a high stone wall hundreds of miles long to keep the winds out, and that's impossible, of course."

"Why?" I asked. "The Chinese built a wall, didn't they?"

"The Chinese, my boy, were great masters."

These childish impressions grew dimmer as the years went by but they did not fade from my memory, now and then, particularly in times of drought, becoming quite vivid and reviving my fears.

When I grew to manhood I became deeply fond of the central part of Russia, my heart won by the fresh green of the landscape, the abundance of clear, cool streams, by the damp forests, drizzling rains and overcast skies. When I saw drought assail this region and parch the land, the fears I previously felt turned into an impotent rage against the desert.

DEVONIAN LIMESTONE

Many years passed before the desert again reminded me of its existence. This was in 1931, when I went to spend the summer in the town of Livni (Oryol Region). I was then writing my first novel and felt drawn to some small town where, not knowing a soul, I could work undisturbed.

I had never before been to Livni. But as soon as I arrived I found the town with its clean streets, heaps of sunflowers, flagstone pavements and the swift-flowing Bistraya Sosna, which had cut a gully in the yellow rock, very much to my liking.

I took lodgings on the outskirts of the town in an old wooden house which stood on a steep bank of the river. Behind the house stretched a half-withered orchard, encroaching on the shrubbery of the river-bank. My landlord was a timid elderly man who had charge of the local railway station's newspaper stand. He had a thin, morose-looking wife and two daughters called Anfisa and Paulina.

Paulina was a frail creature of seventeen, who always spoke shyly to me and played nervously with her blond braids. Anfisa was nineteen, well-built, with a pale face, grave grey eyes and a soft voice. She walked about in black like a novice in a nunnery, avoided housework, and spent long hours lying on the dry grass in the garden and reading. Her books came from the attic, littered with mouse-eaten volumes, mostly Russian editions of world classics. I, too, borrowed these books.

Now and then from the garden I would catch sight of Anfisa sitting on the steep bank of the river near some hawthorn bush. At her side was a sickly, fair-haired, large-eyed youth of about sixteen. I saw Anfisa secretly bring him food, watch him lovingly as he ate it and sometimes pat his hair. Once she quickly covered her face with her hands and burst into a fit of sobbing. The boy stopped eating and looked in alarm at her. I went away quietly and for a long time tried not to think of the scene I had witnessed.

And I had naïvely imagined that in this quiet little town I would be able to cencentrate wholly on the characters and events I was writing about! But here was life itself intruding and upsetting my plans. I knew I would have no peace until I learned what Anfisa's strange behaviour meant. Now I realized that even before I saw her with the boy, her sad eyes contained some hidden secret. And it was revealed to me soon enough.

I was awakened in the middle of the night by thunder. Thunder-storms were frequent in Livni. The inhabitants believed that the town's deposits of iron ore "attracted" storms. Gusts of wind and white flashes of lightning pierced the darkness. Agitated voices came from the adjoining room. "Tell me what law forbids me to love him?" I heard Anfisa demand indignantly. "Show it to me in writing. You've brought me into the world and now you want to kill me. Beasts! He's pining away, burning out like a candle!" she screamed.

"Leave her alone, Mother," I heard my landlord said diffidently to his wife. "Let her have her way, the fool. It's no use arguing with her. But remember, Anfisa, you'll get no money from me. Don't count on that!"

"I don't need your accursed money!" Anfisa retorted. "I'll earn some myself and I'll take him to the Crimea to prolong his life perhaps for another year. I'll run away from home, you'll see. And you won't escape the disgrace of it, I tell you."

I began to realize what was at the bottom of it all. In the hall behind the door someone was snivelling and sobbing. I opened the door and a chance flash of lightning revealed Paulina to me. She stood wrapped in a big shawl with her forehead pressed against the wall.

I called her name quietly. But just then a thunderclap burst with such force that it seemed to drive our cottage underground up to the very roof. Paulina seized my hand with fright.

"Good Lord!" she whispered. "What'll happen now? And there's this storm into the bargain!"

In undertones she confided to me that Anfisa was in love with a boy whose name was Kolya. He was the son of the widow Karpovna, a quiet, inoffensive person who did other people's laundry. Kolya had tuberculosis. It was no use reasoning with the self-willed, high-strung Anfisa. She would have her way or take her life.

The voices in the adjoining room had suddenly died down and Paulina ran off. I went back to bed but kept listening for sounds and could not drop off for a long time. All was quiet in the house. After a while I began to doze to the sound of the dying peals of thunder and the barking of the dogs. Soon I was sound asleep.

I must have been asleep for a long time when I was awakened by my landlord's loud knocking on the door.

"Sorry to disturb you," he said in a dispirited voice, "but there's trouble in the house."

"What's the matter?"

"Anfisa's run away, practically in her nightdress. I'll go to Karpovna. That's the other end of the town. She might be there. Please stay with the family, my wife's fainted."

I dressed hurriedly and, taking some smelling salts, went to revive my landlady. After a while Paulina motioned to me to follow her to the porch. I don't know how to explain these things but somehow I had a strong presentiment of a tragic event.

"Let's go to the river-bank," Paulina said softly.

"Have you got a lantern?"

"Yes."

"Bring it quick!"

Paulina brought a dim lantern and we descended the steep bank down to the river's edge.

"Anfisa-a-a!" Paulina called in dismay. The cry made me start. "It's no use!" I thought, "It's no use!"

Faint streaks of lightning flashed across the sky beyond the river and the thunderclaps now sounded far in the distance. Rain drops rustled in the brushwood on the steep bank. We walked along the river margin following the stream. The light in the lantern was very dim. A flash of lightning lit up the sky just above our heads, and I caught sight of something white on the river-bank.

When I reached the spot I saw a girl's dress, a chemise and a pair of wet shoes.

Paulina screamed and ran back in the direction of the house. I hastened to the ferry and raised the sleeping ferryman. We began crossing and recrossing the river, peering into the water all the time.

"It's useless looking for a body on a stormy night like this," the half-awake ferryman said and yawned. "You won't find it till it's come up to the surface. I remember her, a pretty girl, but death spares no one. That's how it is. Took off her clothes so it would be easier to drown."

Anfisa's dead body was found next morning by the river dam.

In the coffin Anfisa looked very beautiful, her moist

braids the colour of burnished gold and a guilty smile on her pale lips.

"Don't look at her so hard," said an old woman to me. "She's too beautiful, it's enough to break one's heart. Don't look!"

But I couldn't tear my eyes away from Anfisa's face. I knew that it was the first time in my life that I was looking upon the face of a woman whose love was stronger than death. I had previously read about such love in books but had not much believed in its existence. Now for some reason the thought flashed across my mind that such love falls mostly to the lot of Russian women.

Many people came to the funeral. Kolya trailed behind afraid to meet the girl's relatives. Seeing that I was trying to get to him, he quickly gave me the slip.

Anfisa's tragic death affected me greatly. I couldn't go on with my novel. I moved from the outskirts of the town to a squat, somewhat gloomy-looking house by the railway station. The house belonged to Maria Dmitriyevna Shatskaya, a doctor employed in the railway.

Some time before Anfisa drowned herself I happened to be passing through the city park where I noticed a large group of boys sitting on the ground a few steps away from the summer cinema and buzzing with excitement.

A minute later I saw a grey-haired man come out of the cinema and hand out tickets for the show to the delighted youngsters who, yelling and pushing, made a dash for the entrance. The grey-haired man's face was young; I judged him to be no more then forty. Squinting good-naturedly at me, he walked off with a wave of his hand.

I wanted to find out more about this man whose behaviour I thought rather odd and followed the boys to the show. There I spent a dull hour and a half watching an old film called *Red Little Devils* amidst the boys' whistling, banging of feet and shouts of delight and horror.

After the show I gathered the noisy lot of boys around me and succeeded in getting them to tell me all they knew about the man who had treated them to the pictures.

I learned that he was the brother of Dr. Maria Shatskaya, that he was "not quite right in the head" and received a large government pension. What had entitled him to it, no one knew. The pension was brought to him once a month and on that day he bought cinema tickets for the boys of the neighbourhood. The boys made a point of finding out the exact date when the pension was due and would gather in the little garden near the Shatskaya home with an air of being there by chance.

After Anfisa's death my landlady took to her bed, constantly complaining of her heart. Dr. Maria Shatskaya was called to her bedside one day and that is how I made her acquaintance. She was tall, resolute of manner, wore pince-nez and had retained the appearance of a medical student even in her advanced years. She told me that her brother, a geologist by profession, was suffering from a mental disorder. She confirmed what the boys had already told me about his receiving a large pension granted to him for his services in the field of science; his books, she said, had won world recognition.

"This is no place for you," she said to me in a professional tone that brooked no objection. "Autumn is coming, "and it'll be dreadfully muddy here. Besides I'm sure it's impossible to write in such gloomy surroundings. Why not move over to my house? There are only three of us, Mother, brother and myself, and we've got five rooms. We live by the railway station. You needn't fear that my brother will interfere with your work, he is tact itself."

The suggestion pleased me, and thus I made the acquaintance of Vasily Dmitriyevich Shatsky who was to be one of the principal characters of my novel *Kara-Bogaz*.

My new lodgings were very quiet indeed. There was an air of drowsiness about the whole house. Maria Dmitriyevna was out most of the day at the hospital or visiting patients, her old mother sat playing patience and her brother rarely left his room. I noticed that he read the morning paper practically from the first to the last line and spent the rest of the day writing, filling a fat notebook by nightfall. Now and then from the deserted railway station came the whistle of its only locomotive.

At first Vasily Shatsky avoided me, but after a while he got used to my presence and was willing enough to talk. Daily contact with him revealed to me the peculiarities of his illness. In the morning, while his mind was still fresh, his talk was stimulating, differing in no way from that of a normal human being. It was clear that he knew a great deal. But the effects of fatigue would begin to tell on him at once. His mind wandered. Yet he was amazingly logical even in his wanderings.

One day Maria Dmitriyevna showed me her brother's note-book. It contained lines of disconnected words or word combinations, generally beginning with the same letter, with not a single complete sentence among them. These lines read something like this—"Huns, Hohenzollerns, Falsehood, Fraud, Fabrication."

Shatsky never disturbed me when I was writing. Afraid to make a noise, he even walked on tiptoe in the adjoining rooms.

How his mind came to be unhinged I have described in *Kara-Bogaz*. He had gone off on a geological expedition to Central Asia at the time of the Civil War and was captured by Basmachi—counter-revolutionary bandits. Every day along with other captives he was led to the execution ground. But he was lucky: when every fifth man was ordered to be shot, he would always be third, and when it was every second man, he would invariably be first. Thus he survived, but it had cost him his reason. His sister after a long search finally found him in the town of Krasnovodsk living quite alone in a broken-down railway carriage.

Every evening Shatsky took a walk down to the post-office to mail a registered letter addressed to the Council of People's Commissars. Maria Dmitriyevna had a standing arrangement with the postmaster by which he returned her brother's letters to her and she at once burned them.

I was curious to know what Shatsky could write in these letters and was not long in finding out.

"Never put your shoes down with the toes looking forward, it's dangerous," Shatsky said to me one evening as I was lying and reading, and my shoes stood under the bed.

"Why?"

"You'll know in a minute."

He went out and presently returned with a sheet of paper.

"Read it," he said, "and when you're through knock on the wall. If there's anything you don't understand, I'll gladly explain."

He handed me a letter addressed to the Council of People's Commissars.

"I have repeatedly warned you of the grave danger which threatens our Motherland," the opening lines read. "We all know that geological strata contain vast resources of material energy, as for example in deposits of coal, oil and shale," I continued to read what I knew were the ravings of a madman. "Man has learned to release this energy and make use of it.

"But few people are aware of the fact that the brain energy of many ages is stored up in the strata of the earth.

"In the town of Livni are the largest layers of Devonian limestone in Europe. It was in the Devonian Period that the world's dim consciousness, cruel, devoid of the least sign of humanity, was born, a consciousness that was dominated by the sluggish brain of the testacean.

"This rudimentary brain energy is concentrated in rock ammonites. And the layers of Devonian limestone are literally packed with petrified ammonites. Every single ammonite is really a little brain of that long-past age, a receptacle containing the most evil kind of energy.

"Fortunately man has never been able to invent a means of releasing these vast resources of energy. I say 'fortunately,' because if a means were found to release this energy it would be the end of civilization. Human beings infected with its evil power would turn into cruel beasts following blind and base instincts and all culture would be dead.

"But, as I have repeatedly warned the Council of People's Commissars, the fascists have found a means of unleashing the brain energy contained in the Devonian strata and of reviving the ammonites.

"Since there are extremely rich deposits of Devonian limestone in the town of Livni the fascists have chosen it as the centre where they will release the evil brain energy. If they succeed, it will be impossible to avert the moral as well as the physical destruction of the human race."

In his letter Vasily Shatsky went on to say how the fascists had worked out a detailed plan for the release of the brain energy contained in the strata in Livni. But, like all plans, no matter how thorough, the fascists' plan, he said, may fail if just one little screw went wrong, a mere trifle.

"Therefore apart from the necessity of surrounding Livni immediately with large units," Shatsky wrote, "strict orders must be issued to the inhabitants to begin reversing their habits (since the success of the plan depends on the inhabitants being regular in their habits) and to do unexpected things in order to completely baffle the fascists. I shall explain. The citizens of Livni must henceforth when turning in place their shoes by their beds with the heels to the front, instead of the toes. A little thing like that for which the fascists have not made provision may in the end wreck their plans.

74

"Furthermore, I must draw your attention to the fact that little by little the brain energy contained in the Devonian limestone at Livni is escaping from the strata. This has resulted in a deterioration of the morals of this town as compared with other towns of the same type and size.

"I may add in conclusion that the local chemist is the fascists' emissary in Livni."

After having read this letter I was horrified. I realized that Shatsky was not as harmless as he seemed. Soon I discovered that he had frequent fits but that his mother and sister had a way of concealing these from outsiders.

The next evening when we were all seated round the table peacefully discussing homeopathy Shatsky picked up the milk jug and unconcernedly emptied its contents into the pipe of the burning samovar. His mother uttered a cry but Maria Dmitriyevna looked sternly at him.

"At your tricks again?" she said.

With a guilty smile he began to explain that he had poured the milk down the samovar pipe to deceive the fascists, that is to upset their plans and rescue humanity from impending disaster.

"Go to your room at once," his sister ordered in the same stern way. She rose and flung open the windows to let out the fumes of burnt milk, while Vasily Shatsky withdrew from the room very humbly, with bowed head.

In his lucid moments Shatsky spoke eagerly and effusively. I learned that he had spent a good deal of his time in Central Asia and had been one of the first to explore the Kara-Bogaz Bay. In peril of his life, he had ventured along its eastern shores, later describing them and marking them on the map. He had also discovered coal deposits in the rocky mountains near the bay.

He showed me many photographs, such as geologists often take at a great risk to their lives. Among them were pictures of mountains so furrowed by clefts and fissures that they bore an amazing resemblance to the human brain, and of the Ust-Urt tableland ominously rising in a sheer ascent above the desert.

Shatsky was therefore the first to tell me about Kara-Bogaz, this mysterious and dangerous bay in the Caspian, and about its inexhaustible deposits of mirabilite which could be used to transform deserts into flowering lands.

As for the desert, Shatsky hated it as heartily as though it were a living creature. It was, he said, an ulcer, or even a cancer upon the earth's surface, a terrible blight, an inexplicable meanness of nature.

"And the desert must be conquered," he would say to me, "crushed out of existence by our ceaseless, merciless fight and upon its dead body shall rise a land of tropics and rain."

My dormant hatred for the desert, an echo of my childhood days, was revived by his words.

"If but half the money and energy that is spent on wars would be used for fighting the desert," he continued, "there would be no desert areas today. War drains our national wealth, it carries off millions of human lives. And science, culture, even poetry abet in this slaughter of mankind."

"Vasily," Maria Dmitriyevna's loud voice came from the adjoining room. "Compose yourself. There will be no more wars. Never!"

"Nonsense!" said Shatsky in a changed tone. "This very night the ammonites will come to life. And I'll tell you the exact place: near the flour-mill. We can go there and see for ourselves."

He was beginning to rave. Maria Dmitriyevna led him away, gave him a sedative and got him into bed.

There was one thought uppermost in my mind—to finish the novel I was writing as quickly as possible, and to begin a new one about man's struggle to turn deserts into fertile lands. Thus *Kara-Bogaz* which I wrote some time later was taking shape in my mind.

It was late autumn when I left Livni. Before my departure I went to say good-bye to Anfisa's family. I found the old woman still in bed and my former landlord out. Paulina walked with me back to town.

It was dusk. The thin ice crackled underfoot. Except for a shrivelled leaf here and there, the fruit-trees were bare. The last cloud faded in the cold setting sun.

Paulina walked by my side and put her hand trustfully into mine. This made her seem quite a little girl to me, lonely and shy, and a deep tenderness for her filled my heart.

As we approached the town, muffled strains of music reached us from a nearby cinema. Lights began to twinkle in the cottages and the smoke of samovars curled over the orchards. In between the leafless boughs the stars gleamed bright.

A strange agitation gripped my heart and I thought that for the sake of the beautiful land around me, even for the sake of a lovely girl like Paulina, human beings must be urged to fight for a happy and rational existence. All that brought misery and grief to the human race must be uprooted: deserts, wars, injustice, falsehood, and scorn for the human heart.

Paulina accompanied me as far as the first town buildings. Casting down her eyes and playing with her braid she said unexpectedly: "I'm going to read a great deal now, Konstantin Grigoryevich." She glanced shyly at me. We shook hands and she quickly walked away.

To Moscow I travelled in a crowded carriage. At night I went out for a smoke to the platform, lowered the window and put my head out.

The train was speeding along a bank with woods on either side. The woods were wrapped in shadow but I could divine their presence from the echo of the train's rumble in the thickets. A chill blast blew into my face

77

bringing with it the odour of early snow and frost-bitten foliage. Overhead, keeping pace with the train, the autumn sky glided, dazzling in the brilliance of its stars. Bridges rattled under the moving wheels of the train; the flash of stars was caught in the murky water of passing creeks and streams.

And the train clattered and rumbled and puffed, with flickering headlights and flying sparks, the engine whistling for all its worth, as though intoxicated with its own rolling speed.

I felt the train was bringing me to some great fulfilment. The idea for my new novel was expanding in my brain. I knew now that I would write it.

Leaning out of the window I began to sing in disconnected words of the beauties of the night and of my deep attachment to the land of my birth. The wind's caress against my face was like that of a young girl's sweet-smelling braids. I longed to kiss the braids, the wind and the cold moist earth below. Unable to do that I sang like one possessed, uttering meaningless words and delighting in the beauty of the eastern sky where a faint delicate blue was now breaking through the darkness. I only half realized that a new day was dawning.

The views I saw and the exhilaration I felt combined in some subtle way to make me resolve to write, to write at once. But what to write? I knew that my meditations on the beauties of the land and my passionate longing to save that land from exhaustion and death would mould themselves into a theme—what that theme would be was immaterial to me.

And my thoughts soon took definite shape in the idea for the novel which I later called *Kara-Bogaz*. They could easily have found expression in an idea for a different book. Yet it would have to be saturated with the very emotions and thoughts that possessed me at the time.

This makes me believe that an idea for a book almost always springs from the heart.

With the idea there, a new period for the writer sets in, the "breeding" period, or rather the period of clothing the idea in material gleaned from life.

STUDYING MAPS

On arriving in Moscow I obtained a detailed map of the Caspian Sea and for a long time roamed (in my imagination, of course) over its arid eastern shores.

Maps had fascinated me since my childhood and I would pore over them for long hours as if they were the most thrilling books. I studied the direction of rivers, and the curiously indented coastlines, the taiga where trading centres were marked by tiny circles, and repeated as one repeats lines of poetry such fine-sounding geographical names as the Hebrides, Guadarrama Mountains, Inverness, Lake Onega and the Cordilleras.

Gradually I came to have such a vivid picture of these places in my mind that I could easily have composed traveller's notes on many parts of the globe.

Even my romantically-minded father did not approve of my excessive interest in geography, saying that it held many disappointments for me.

"If in later life you get the opportunity to travel, you are bound to be disillusioned," he said. "You will find the countries you visit quite different from what you imagined them to be. Mexico, for example, may turn out to be dusty and poverty-stricken, and the equatorial skies grey and dull."

I did not believe him. The sky above the equator I knew could never be grey. To me it was a deep blue so that even the snows of Kilimanjaro took on an indigo hue.

In any case my interest in geography did not flag. Later, when I had occasion to travel, my conviction that Father's view was far from right was corroborated.

There was the Crimea. True, when I paid my first visit there (and before that I had studied every bit of it on the map) it was different from the land of my imagination. Yet the fact that I had already formed a picture of the country in my mind made me a much keener observer than if I had had no previous idea of it at all. Everywhere I found features which my imagination had missed and those features impressed themselves most strongly on my memory.

The same holds good for the impression produced by people. All of us, for example, have some idea of what Gogol was like. But could we get a glimpse of Gogol in the flesh, we would notice many traits which did not tally with the Gogol of our imagination. And these traits, I think, would strike us most. On the other hand, if we did not have a preconceived idea of the writer, we would probably miss a great deal that was worthy of our attention. Most of us imagine Gogol glum, high-strung, and phlegmatic. Hence features that contradict this mental picture of Gogol would stand out all the more—that is when we found him to be unexpectedly bright-eyed, vivacious, even somewhat fidgety, with an inclination to laugh, elegantly dressed and speaking with a strong Ukrainian accent.

Evasive as these thoughts may be I am nevertheless convinced of their correctness.

Thus, studying a land on the map and travelling through it in our imagination, colours it with a certain romance, and if we later come to visit it we are not likely ever to find it dull.

When I arrived in Moscow I was already roaming in my imagination on the bleak shores of the Caspian. At the same time I read everything I could lay my hands on in the Lenin Library about the desert—fiction, travel stories, treatises and even Arabian poems. I read Przhevalsky, Anuchin, Sven Hedin, Vámbéry, MacGaham,

Grum-Grzhimailo, Shevchenko's diaries on Mangyshlak peninsula, the history of Khiva and Bukhara, Butakov's reports, the works of the explorer Karelin, and various geological surveys. And what I read—the fruit of man's stubborn probings—opened up a wonderful world to me.

Finally the time came for me to go and see the Caspian and Kara-Bogaz for myself, but I had no money.

I went to one of the publishing houses and spoke to the manager, telling him I was writing a novel about Kara-Bogaz Bay. I hoped for a contract but his reaction was far from enthusiastic.

"You must have completely lost touch with Soviet reality to suggest anything so preposterous," he said.

"Why?"

"Because the only interesting thing about Kara-Bogaz Bay is that it has Glauber salt deposits. You don't seriously propose to write a novel about a purgative, do you? If you're not making fun of me and are in earnest, get that crazy idea out of your head. You won't find a single publisher that'll advance you a kopek on it."

With great difficulty I managed to procure some money from other sources.

I went to Saratov and from there down the Volga to Astrakhan. Here I got stranded, having spent the little sum of money I had. By writing a few stories for an Astrakhan newspaper and for *Thirty Days*, a Moscow magazine, I scraped together the fare for further travels.

To write the stories I took a trip up the Emba River and to the Astrakhan steppes which proved very helpful in my work on the novel. To reach the Emba I sailed on the Caspian past shores thickly overgrown with reeds. The old boat had a strange name—*Heliotrope*. Like on most old vessels there was much brass in evidence everywhere—brass hand-rails, compasses, binoculars, ship's instruments and even the cabin thresholds were of brass.

It all made the *Heliotrope* look like a polished, smoking samovar tossing about on the small waves of a shallow sea.

Seals floated on their backs in the warm water, now and then sluggishly flapping their fins. Young girls in navy blue sailor suits, with fish scales sticking to their faces, came on rafts and followed the *Heliotrope* with their laughter and whistling.

Reflections of the creamy clouds overhead and the white sandy islands around us mingled indistinguishably in the shimmering water. The little town of Guryev rose in a pall of smoke. I boarded a brand-new train, making its first trip, and rode to the Emba through steppe country. Oil pumps wheezed in the town of Dossor on the Emba amidst lakes with pink glossy water. There was a pungent odour of brine. In place of window-panes the town's houses had metal nets so thickly covered with midges that no light could penetrate.

When I reached the Emba I became wholly absorbed in oil-extraction, learning all I could about oil derricks, oil-prospecting in the desert, heavy oil and light oil, the famous oil-fields of Maracaibo in Venezuela, where oil engineers from the Emba went for additional experience. I saw a solpugid bite one of the oil engineers. The next day he died.

This was Central Asia. It was sweltering hot. The stars twinkled through a haze of dust. Old Kazakhs walked about the streets in flowing calico trousers with gaudy patterns of black peonies and green leaves against a pink background.

After each trip I returned to Astrakhan. I lived in a little wooden house belonging to a journalist who worked for the Astrakhan daily paper. On my arrival in the city he had made me come and stay with him. I felt very much at ease in his house which stood on the bank of a canal in a little garden full of blooming nasturtiums. It was in this garden, in a tiny bower with no more room than for one person, that I wrote my stories for the paper. And there I slept, too.

The journalist's wife, a kind, sickly-looking young woman, spent a good deal of the day in the kitchen quietly weeping over the garments of her baby which had died two months before.

After my stories were written in Astrakhan, my journalist's work took me to other towns—Makhach-Kala, Baku and Krasnovodsk. Some of my later experiences are described in *Kara-Bogaz*. I returned to Moscow, but a few days afterwards was travelling again as a correspondent in the North Urals—in the towns of Berezniki and Solikamsk. After the unbelievable heat of Asia, I found myself in a land of dark pine-woods, bogs, hills covered with lichen and of early winter.

In Solikamsk, in a monastery converted into a hotel, I began to write *Kara-Bogaz*. Wartime-fashion, I shared my dreary cold vaulted room with three other occupants. They were chemical engineers—two women and a man—employed at the potassium mines in Solikamsk. There was a 17th-century air about the hotel—a smell of incense, bread, and animal hides. Night watchmen in sheepskin coats struck the hour on iron plates, and alabaster cathedrals, built at the time of the wealthy Stroganovs, loomed white in the dismal light of falling snow. There was nothing here to remind me of Central Asia. And that for some reason made it easier for me to write.

That is a brief, hasty sketch of how I came to write my novel *Kara-Bogaz*. In it, of course, I have omitted many of the encounters, the trips, the conversations and incidents which have been woven into the fabric of my story. On the other hand, not all of the material I accumulated was incorporated in the book, which is not to be regretted, for it may well come in handy for some future novel.

While writing *Kara-Bogaz* I made use of what I had seen during my trips along the shores of the Caspian with little regard to plan or structure. When the novel appeared my critics spoke of it as having a "spiral composition" and seemed quite happy about it. I must admit that when I wrote it I did not give much thought to the composition.

What I did think about a great deal was that I should not miss the romance and heroic spirit that lend a glow to the commonplace and must be expressed vividly and faithfully—be it a novel about Glauber salt or about the construction of a paper-mill in the forests of the North.

If he wishes to move human hearts the writer must worship truth, must have deep faith in man's reason and a keen love of life.

The other day I read a poem by Pavel Antokolsky. In it are two verses which well express the state of one who is in love with life. I quote them here:

> *The distant sighs of violins*
> *Proclaiming sway of Spring that's nigh,*
> *And silence, ringing crystalline*
> *With countless drops, the call replying.*
>
> *And all these melodies of nature,*
> *Which time is helpless to destroy,*
> *Will live untainted through the ages,*
> *To fill the hearts of men with joy.*

THE HEART REMEMBERS

The heart's memory is mightier
than the sad memory of reason.

BATYUSHKOV

 eaders often ask writers how and over what period they collect the material for a novel or a story. They are surprised when told that there was no deliberate collecting of material at all. This does not, of course, apply to books of a strictly factual and scientific aspect. By "material" I mean *life* or, as Dostoyevsky termed it, "the little things that make up life."

Life is not really studied by the writer but *lived* by him. We may say that writers live *inside* their material. They suffer, think, enjoy themselves, take part in the life around them. Every day leaves its mark. And the heart remembers.

The notion that the writer is someone who flits about the world carefully jotting down everything he may need for his future books is wrong.

Of course, there are writers who make it a point to take notes and store up random observations. But such observations can never be mechanically transferred from the pad into the pattern of a book. They will not fit in.

And so for the writer to go about life saying to himself: "I must study that cluster of ashberries, or that nice grey-haired drummer in the orchestra, or somebody or something because I might need them professionally at some later date" is not of much use.

Artificial squeezing in of even the most interesting observations into a piece of writing will lead to no good. Observations have a way of getting into the writer's story at the right moment and in the right place of their own accord. Indeed, writers find not without surprise that long-forgotten experiences crop up just at the time when they are most needed. A good memory is therefore one of the writer's greatest assets.

Perhaps if I describe how I came to write *The Telegram*, one of my short stories, I may be able to make my point clearer.

Late in the autumn I went to stay in a village near Ryazan. There I took lodgings in a house which had once belonged to a famous engraver. My landlady, Ekaterina Ivanovna Pozhalostina, was the engraver's daughter, a kind, frail old lady in the evening of a lonely old age. She had a daughter called Nastya who lived in Leningrad and remembered her mother only to send her a small allowance once in two months.

I occupied a room in this big empty house with its age-blackened log walls. To communicate with Ekaterina Ivanovna I needed to cross a hall and several rooms with squeaky, dusty floor-boards. The sole occupants of this house, which was of historical interest because of its late owner, were the old lady and myself.

Beyond the courtyard with its dilapidated outbuildings was a large orchard, neglected as was the house itself, damp and chilly, with the wind whistling among the trees.

This new place was my retreat; I came here to write. At first my routine was to work from morning till dusk; it went dark early so that by five o'clock the old oil-lamp with its tulip-shaped glass shade had to be lit. Later I began to work in the evening, preferring to spend the few hours of daylight outdoors, roaming in the woods and fields.

Everywhere on my rambles I saw the signs of late autumn. In the morning a thin crust sheathed the pools of water with spurting air bubbles in which, as in a hollow crystal, lay birch and aspen leaves, touched by crimson or golden yellow. I would break the ice and pick up these frost-bitten leaves and carry them home with me. Very soon I had a whole heap of them on my window-sill, warm now and smelling of spirits.

Best of all I liked to wander through the woods, where it was not as windy as in the open fields and where there was a sombre tranquillity broken only by the crackling of thin ice. It was quiet and dismal there—perhaps because of the dark clouds drifting so low over the earth that the crowns of the stately birches were as often as not wrapped in mist.

Sometimes I went angling in the streams of the Oka, among impassable thickets with an acrid, penetrating odour of willow leaves that seemed to nip the skin of the face. The water was black with dull green tints and, as is always the case in late autumn, the fish were slow to bite.

Soon the rains came, setting the orchard in disarray, beating the faded grass down to the ground and filling the air with a smell of sleet.

The signs of late autumn and approaching winter were

many, but I made no effort to commit them to memory. Yet I felt convinced that I would never forget that autumn with its bitter tang which in some strange way raised my spirits and cleared my head.

The drearier the drift of broken rain-clouds, the colder the rains, the lighter my heart became, and the freer the words flowed from my pen.

It was to get the feel of that autumn, the train of thought and emotions it aroused, that was important. All the rest, all that we call "material"—people, events, details—was, I knew, wrapped up in that feeling. And should it revive at some later time while I am writing all the rest would come with it ready for me to put it on paper.

I did not make a point of studying the old house as material for a story. I merely learned to love it for its dismal appearance and for its quiet, for the uneven ticking of its old clock, for the odour of burning birch logs in the stove and the old engravings on the walls—there were very few left in the house now, almost all had been taken to the local museum—such as Bryullov's *Self-Portrait, Bearing of the Cross* and Perov's *Bird-Catcher*, and a portrait of Pauline Viardot.

The window-panes, age-worn and crooked, gleamed with all the colours of the rainbow and in the evening a double reflection of the candle flame played in them. All the furniture—the sofas, tables and chairs—was of light-coloured wood, with a time-worn patina and a cypress scent reminiscent of icons.

There were quite a few curious objects, such as torch-shaped copper night-lights, secret locks, round jars of age-hardened creams with Paris labels, a small dust-covered wax nosegay of camellias (suspended from a huge rusty nail) and a round little brush for rubbing off the scores chalked on the card table.

There were also three calendars, dated 1848, 1850 and 1852. Attached to them were lists of ladies of the Russian

court. I found the name of Pushkin's wife, Natalia Niko-
layevna Lanskaya, and that of Elizaveta Ksaveryevna
Vorontsova, whom the poet had once dearly loved. A sadness possessed me why I cannot tell. Perhaps because of
the unearthly stillness of the house. Far away on the Oka,
near the Kuzminsky sluice, the steamer's siren sounded
shrilly, and the lines which Pushkin wrote for Vorontsova kept revolving in my mind:

The dismal day has waned. The night with dismal
gloom
Is spreading now its leaden robes across the skies,
And like a ghost, beyond the grove of pines,
Appears the pale and misty moon.

In the evening I had tea with Ekaterina Ivanovna. Her
sight was failing her and Nyurka, a neighbour's girl who
came to do some of the housework, helped prepare the samovar. Nyurka had a glum and sulky disposition. As she
joined us at the table, she drank her tea noisily out of a
saucer. To all that Ekaterina Ivanovna said in her soft
voice, Nyurka had but one comment to make: "To be
sure! Tell me some more!"

When I tried to put her to shame she only said: "To be
sure! You think me dull, but I'm not!"

However Nyurka was the only creature who was sincerely attached to Ekaterina Ivanovna. Her loving the old
lady had nothing to do with the odd gifts she received
from her now and then, such as an outmoded velvet hat
trimmed with a stuffed humming-bird, a beaded cap, or
bits of lace grown yellow with age.

In years long past Ekaterina Ivanovna had lived in
Paris with her father. There she had met many interesting people, among them Turgenev. She had also attended Victor Hugo's funeral. She told me of all this, her

words punctuated by Nyurka's invariable, "To be sure! Tell me some more!"

Nyurka never stayed up late with us as she had to hurry home to put "the little ones" to bed, meaning her younger brothers and sisters.

Ekaterina Ivanovna always carried about herself a worn little satin bag. It contained all her most precious possessions, a little money, her passport, Nastya's letters and photograph, showing her to be a handsome woman with delicately curved eyebrows and dim eyes, and a photograph of herself as a young girl on which she looked as sweet and pure as any young creature can possibly look.

From what I knew of Ekaterina Ivanovna she never complained of anything but her old age. However from talks with the neighbours and with Ivan Dmitriyevich, a kind old muddle-headed watchman, I learned that Ekaterina Ivanovna suffered greatly because her only daughter was anything but thoughtful of her mother. For four years she had not paid a single visit to Ekaterina Ivanovna whose days were now numbered. And Ekaterina Ivanovna could not bear the thought of dying without seeing Nastya, whose "wonderful blond hair" she longed so to touch.

One day she asked me to take her into the garden. Because of her ill health, she had not ventured there since early spring.

"You don't mind taking an old woman like me out, do you?" she asked. "I want to see, perhaps for the last time, the garden where as a girl I loved to pore over Turgenev's novels. I planted some of the trees myself."

Wrapped up in a warm coat and shawl, which it took her a long time to adjust, she slowly came down the steps of the porch, leaning on my arm.

Dusk was gathering. The garden had shed all of its foliage and the fallen leaves hampered our steps, stirring and crackling underfoot. The first star gleamed in the greenish sunset. Above a distant wood the moon's crescent hung in the sky.

Ekaterina Ivanovna paused to rest by a wind-battered linden, supporting herself with her hand against it, and began to weep.

Fearing that she might fall, I held her tightly. The tears ran down her cheeks and, like most very old people, she was unashamed of them.

"May the Lord spare you a lonely old age like mine, my dear," she said at last.

Gently I accompanied her into the house, thinking that if only I had a mother like her I would be the happiest man on earth.

That same evening Ekaterina Ivanovna gave me a bundle of letters, yellow with age, which had belonged to her father. Among them I found letters of the famous Russian painter Kramskoi and of engraver Iordan from Rome. The latter wrote of his friendship with Thorwaldsen, the great Danish sculptor, and of Lateran's wonderful marble statues.

I read the letters, as was my custom, at night, with the wind howling through the wet, bare bushes outdoors, and the lamp humming as though talking to itself out of sheer boredom. The night was cold and rainy. The collective-farm watchman kept sounding his rattle. In this atmosphere I found reading the letters from Rome a strange but pleasant occupation. They awakened in me an interest in the personality of Thorwaldsen. When I returned to Moscow I set about finding out all I could concerning him. I discovered that he had been a close friend of Hans Christian Andersen and it all led me several years later to write a short story about Andersen. So it was really the old house that had set me off on the story.

Some days after we had been in the garden Ekaterina Ivanovna took to her bed for good. She complained of nothing except a general weariness. I sent a telegram to Nastya in Leningrad. Nyurka moved into Ekaterina Ivanovna's rooms in order to be close at hand.

Late one night I was awakened by Nyurka banging on the wall.

"Come quickly, she's dying!" the girl screamed in a frightened voice.

I found Ekaterina Ivanovna in a coma, with hardly any breath left in her sinking body. A feeble quivering had replaced the regular beats of the pulse, which was now as fragile as a cobweb.

Taking a lantern I hurried to the village hospital to fetch a doctor. My way lay through pitch-black woods with the wind bringing the smell of sawdust to my nostrils—obviously there was tree-felling going on. The hour was late, for the dogs had ceased their barking.

After making a camphor injection, the doctor said with a sigh that there was no hope for Ekaterina Ivanovna, but as her heart was strong, she would hold out for a while. Ekaterina Ivanovna breathed her last in the morning. I was at her side to close her eyes, and I saw a great big tear roll down her cheeks as I gently pressed the lids down.

Nyurka, choking with tears, handed me a crumpled envelope.

"There's a note left by Ekaterina Ivanovna," she said.

I tore open the envelope and read a few words written in an unsteady hand—a bare statement of what Ekaterina Ivanovna wished to be buried in. I gave the note to some women who came to dress the body in the morning.

After returning from the cemetery where I had picked a plot for the grave, I found Ekaterina Ivanovna already lying on the table dressed for her last journey. I was surprised to see her looking as slim as a young girl, in a quaint old-fashioned ball dress of golden yellow, its long train loosely draped around her legs, and tiny suede slippers peeping out from under it. Her hands, holding a candle, were in tight white kid gloves reaching to her elbows and a nosegay of red satin roses was pinned to her bodice. A veil covered her face. If it had not been for the shrivelled elbows showing between the sleeves and the gloves, one could easily have taken her for a beautiful young woman.

Nastya, her daughter, missed the funeral by three days.

All the above is material which goes into the making of a piece of writing.

It is interesting to note that the whole atmosphere in which I found myself—the neglected house and the autumn scene—was strangely symbolic of the tragedy of Ekaterina Ivanovna's last days.

But, of course, a good deal of what I saw and pondered over did not go into my story *The Telegram* at all, and it could not have been otherwise.

For a short story the writer needs copious material from which to select that which is most significant and essential.

I have watched talented actors working on minor parts, containing perhaps no more than two or three lines. These actors took the trouble of finding out all they could from the playwright about the character they had to portray—extra details about appearance, life and background—in their eagerness to bring out all the force in the few lines they had.

The same is true of the writer. The material he draws upon is far in excess of that which he actually uses in the story.

I have told how I came to write *The Telegram*, which shows that every story has its material and a history of its own.

I recall a winter I spent in Yalta. Whenever I opened the windows wind-blown withered oak leaves came scuttling across the floor. They were not leaves of century-old oaks but of saplings which grow abundantly in Crimea's mountain pastures. At night a cold blast blew from the mountains sheated in gleaming snow.

Aseyev, who lived next door, was writing a poem about heroic Spain (it was at the time of the Civil War in Spain) and "Barcelona's ancient skies," while the poet Vladimir Lugovskoi sang old English sailor songs in his powerful bass. In the evenings we would gather round the radio to hear the latest news from the Spanish front.

We paid a visit to the observatory in Simeiz, near Yalta, where a grey-haired astronomer showed us the illimitable spaces of the universe swarming with stars dazzling in their brilliance, while the refractors with their clanging clock mechanisms kept shifting under the cupola of the observatory.

Now and then gunfire from warships on manoeuvres in the Black Sea reached Yalta, causing the water in the carafe to splash. Its muffled roar carried across the mountain meadows and died in the woods. At night planes droned overhead.

I had a book on Cervantes by Bruno Frank and as there were not many books about I re-read it several times.

At that time the swastika was spreading its tentacles over Europe. Germany's most noble minds and hearts were fleeing the country, among them Heinrich Mann, Einstein, Remarque and Stephan Zweig; they were not going to lend their support to the brown plague and to Hitler, the homocidal maniac. But they took with them their unshakable faith in the triumph of humanism.

Arkady Gaidar, also my neighbour, brought home one day a huge sheep-dog with laughing light brown eyes.

At that time he was writing *The Blue Cup,* one of his most wonderful stories. He pretended to know nothing about literature. It was one of his pet foibles.

In the night the roar of the Black Sea was plaintive and far more audible than by day, and my writing flowed easily to its music.

What I have written is an attempt to sketch hazily the atmosphere which worked itself into *The Constellation,* a short story. Practically everything I have mentioned—the dry oak leaves, a grey-haired astronomer, the gunfire, Cervantes, people with unshakable faith in the triumph of humanism, a sheep-dog, planes flying at night—went into the making of my story. But the key-note, and what I tried hardest to convey to the reader and to feel myself throughout the writing of the story, was the cold blast blowing from the mountains at night.

TREASURY OF RUSSIAN WORDS

> One wonders at the preciousness of
> our language: the sounds are like jew-
> els; everything is grainy and weighty
> like real pearls and the name of a
> thing is at times more precious than
> the thing itself.

NIKOLAI GOGOL

SPRING IN A COPSE

any Russian words radiate poetry in the
same way as precious stones radiate a
mysterious glow.

I understand, of course, that there is nothing mysterious about the play of lights
in stones, for it can easily be explained by
the physicist as one of the laws of optics. But it is none-
theless hard to disassociate the sparkle and glitter of
gems from a sensation of the mysterious, and hard to
believe that the gems have not their own source of radiat-
ing light.

This is true when we look at any precious stone, even
the modest aquamarine whose true colour it is so difficult
to define. Its name suggests the bluish and greenish
tints of sea-water. But the great charm of the aquamarine is its inner gleam of pure silver which, when you

look deep into it, reveals smooth sea-water the colour of stars.

It is this magic play of light and colour inside the aquamarine and in other stones that lends them mystery and their beauty seems to us inexplicable.

To explain the power of words whose meaning suggests something poetic is perhaps not so very difficult. It is far more difficult to define the power of words which by their sound alone evoke poetic images. An example of such a word is *зарница* (zarnitsa), meaning "summer lightning." Its sound conveys a picture of lingering flashes of far-off lightning in a warm night.

Of course, our reaction to words is purely subjective, and I shall speak here of my own sensations. But it can be taken as a general truth that most Russian words having a poetic aura are in some way connected with nature.

The spoken language of the common people particularly abounds in these words. And it may be said of the Russian language in general that it will reveal the truly magic power of its words and all its richness only to him who is in closest touch with the people and responds to the beauties of his native land. Russian is a language extremely rich in words and expressions bearing on the phenomena of nature, such as water, air, sky, clouds, sun, rain, forest, marshes, lakes, plains and meadows, flowers and grasses.

The language of the writers famous in Russian literature for their descriptions of nature—Kaigorodov, Prishvin, Gorky, Alexei Tolstoi, Aksakov, Leskov, Bunin and others—must be studied; but even more so one must know the language as it is spoken by the people. I mean our collective farmers, our raftsmen, shepherds, beekeepers, hunters, fishermen, factory workers, forest rangers, buoy-keepers, artisans, village painters and all worldly-wise people whose every word is worth its weight in gold.

A talk I once had with a forest ranger illustrates very well the point I wish to make in this chapter.

This forest ranger and I were walking through a copse which long ago had been a great big marsh. As the years went by the marsh dried up, grass began to grow, and today the only traces of the marsh were the deep, century-old moss, the over-grown pools and the abundance of marsh tea plants.

I do not share the contempt that many have for young woods. Small trees have a charm of their own. It is a pleasure to watch saplings of all kinds, such as pine, asp, fir and birch, grow quickly in dense clumps. In a copse it is never gloomy as it is in a dense forest but sunny and cheerful like in a smiling peasant hut before a holiday.

Whenever I am in a copse, I can't help thinking that it must have been in just such a place that the painter Nesterov found inspiration for his wonderful landscapes. Here every stalk and twig has individuality.

Walking through the copse, we would now and then come across a pool in the deep moss. The water at first glance seemed stagnant, but on closer inspection we could see at the bottom a fresh spring with dry bilberry leaves and yellow pine needles whirling in it. At one we stopped for a drink. The water smelt of turpentine.

"There is a spring here," said the forest ranger as we watched a furiously wriggling little beetle come up to the surface and then quickly sink to the bottom again. "Perhaps the Volga has its source in just such a spring."

"Perhaps," I agreed.

"I like puzzling over words, it's a hobby of mine," the forest ranger said unexpectedly with an embarrassed smile. "It sometimes happens that a word sticks in your head and gives you no peace."

He paused adjusting the rifle across his shoulder and asked:

"They say you're a writer?"

"So I am."

"That means you know a good deal about words. As to me, no matter how much I think about words, I can rarely explain the origin of a word. I keep turning over different words in my mind on my rounds in the forest. How they came to be—I don't know. That's because I've had no education. But then at times it seems to me that I've hit on the right solution, and I'm delighted. And why it should give me so much pleasure puzzles me, too. After all, I'm not a schoolmaster to explain things to kids, I'm just an ignorant forest ranger."

"And is any word bothering you at present?"

"Yes the word *родник* (rodnik—spring). It's a word that's been giving me trouble for a long time. I guess it's spring because water springs from it. From the spring springs a river—(rodnik rodit reku)—and rivers flow through the length and breadth of our Motherland (*rod*ina) and help feed our people (na*rod*). See how all the words have the same root—*rod*nik, *rod*ina, na*rod,* and are of one family (*rod*nya—kin)."

This conversation revealed to me how susceptible we all are to the power of suggestion contained in language.

LANGUAGE AND NATURE

I am certain that the writer must be in touch with nature if he wishes to deepen his knowledge of words and develop his feeling for the Russian language. Being in the fields and woods, among streams and age-old willows, with the birds twittering and the flowers nodding under every bush, will sharpen his language sense.

There is, I suppose, a period in the life of most people when they are happy in the discoveries they make. I experienced this one summer in the woodlands and meadows of Central Russia. It was a summer rich in rainstorms and rainbows.

That summer brings back to me the murmur of the pine-woods, the jabbering of the crane, billows of drifting clouds, the starry brilliance of nocturnal skies, fragrant thickets of meadow-sweet, the cocks' battle cries, and the singing of young girls in the gathering dusk with the glow of the sunset gilding their eyes and the early fog rising gently over the pools.

It was during that summer that many Russian words, long familiar yet evidently insufficiently understood, revealed themselves to me in their full meaning. It was as though I began to know them to the touch, taste and smell. Formerly they merely suggested the vague image of something. Now they were invested with a wealth of living images.

Among the words that I thus made so much my own —and their name was legion—were, for example, many describing rain. There is drizzling rain, driving rain, pelting rain, rain that comes in flurries, torrents and in sheets, sun-showers, slanting rain, and so on. While all these words describing rain were familiar to me before, close contact with nature, seeing constantly the different kinds of rains, made their mention now bring a far more vivid picture to my mind.

By the way, there is a law governing the power of the words the writer uses. That power is proportionate to what the writer himself sees behind the words. If the writer sees nothing behind his own words and phrases, you may be sure the reader will not see anything behind them either. But if the writer has a vivid picture of the word he uses, that word, even if it is a hackneyed one, will have amazing power over the reader and will evoke the thoughts, associations and emotions which the writer hoped so very much to convey. Therein lies the secret of the writer's between-the-lines commentary.

But I haven't done with rain yet. First of all, there are the many signs by which we can tell that it is going to rain: the sun hides behind the clouds, the smoke drifts downwards, the swallows fly low and the clouds are strung across the sky in long gloomy shreds. And before it begins to rain, and the clouds are not yet heavily laden, there is a delicate breath of moisture in the air, coming perhaps from places where it had already rained.

A single adjective may suffice for the writer to convey to the reader's mind some particular kind of rain. When we speak of pelting rain, the picture we at once get is of rain coming down hard with an ever-increasing patter. It is particularly fascinating to watch pelting rain falling in the river. You can see each drop forming a tiny eddy, bouncing up then down again and glistening like a pearl. The rain fills the air with its tinkling sound. And by its sound we know whether it is coming down heavier or abating.

Now, a fine dense rain is different. It drops sleepily from low driving clouds and leaves warm puddles. Practically soundless, except for a soft, somnolent murmuring, it falls steadily, trickling down the bushes and gently washing the leaves one by one. The mossy forest soil absorbs it slowly but surely. And that is why after this kind of rain all manner of mushrooms begin to grow. No wonder we call this rain "mushroom rain" (gribnoi dozhd) in Russian. During such a rain there is an odour of smoke; the roaches, usually shrewd and wary, bite readily.

Who has not found it fascinating during a shower to watch the play of light and listen to the change in sound, ranging from the even beat of the rain on wooden roofs, and a trickling of the water down the pipes, to the unbroken drumming of a heavy downpour with the water coming down in sheets?

So you see the subject of rain offers endless possibilities to the writer. But not all writers are as enthusiastic about nature and its various manifestations as I am. A fellow-writer of mine once tried to damp my enthusiasm.

"Nature bores me," he said, "it is dead, I prefer the teeming streets of our towns. All I can say about rain is that I hate to be out in it and that it is one of the inconveniences of life. You, my friend, are letting your imagination run away with you."

FLOWERS AND GRASS

The forest ranger I mentioned was not the only one who found puzzling over words and their meanings a fascinating game. A good many people I know, myself included, like racking their brains over words.

I remember how hard I had once tried to guess the meaning and trace the origin of an unfamiliar word I had come across in one of Yesenin's poems. Of course, it was not to be found in the dictionary. But its sound somehow suggested to me its approximate meaning and I found it extremely poetic—that is often the case with Russian words. The real meaning and origin of this word I learned later from the writer Yurin who came to visit me on the shores of the Oka where I was living at the time. This writer was an unusual person. He had made a close study of everything connected with Central Russia—geography, flora and fauna, history and local dialects. And after I had learned all I could about the word that had puzzled me, I was as delighted as my forest ranger friend would have been. Possibly the word in question was coined by Sergei Yesenin. It meant the rippling of sand by the wind, something one sees very often on the banks of the Oka; and Yesenin was born not far from the Oka in the village of Konstantinovka (now called Yesenino).

One day Yurin and I went for a stroll through the fields and along the banks of the river. Across the river lay Yesenin's native village, hidden from view by the steep bank. The sun had set beyond the village. And ever since nothing seems to me to give a better picture of the Oka's far-flung sunsets, the twilight in the damp meadows, wrapped in mist or in the bluish smoke from forest fires, than Yesenin's poetry.

In the meadows around the Oka, quiet and deserted, I have had some interesting experiences and encounters.

I happened to be fishing in a small lake enclosed by steep banks overgrown with gristly bramble. The age-old willows and black poplars stood sentinel over the lake and it was always windless and shady there even on a bright sunny day. I sat at the verge of the water, the tall grass almost completely concealing me from the bank. Around the lake's edge yellow irises bloomed. Some distance away on the dull surface of the water little air bubbles kept rising up from the bottom of the lake making me think that carps must be searching for food there. On the bank, where the flowers grew waist-high, some of the village children were gathering sorrel. Judging by the voices there were three girls and a little boy.

The children were playing some sort of game in which two of the girls made believe that they were grown-ups with big families, obviously imitating their own mothers in manner and speech. The third girl did not seem to take an interest in the game. She was singing a song, repeating over and over again only two lines of it, and mispronouncing one of the words.

"Aren't you ashamed of yourself?" said one of the two girls who pretended to be a grown-up. "Here I slave all day long to send you to school. And what do they teach you at school if you get all your words wrong, I'd like to know? Wait till I tell your father, he'll give it you!"

"My son Petya's brought a bad mark from school," chimed in the other girl. "I spanked him so hard that my hands still ache."

"You're a fibber, Nyurka," said the little boy in a husky voice. "*Mummy* spanked me, not you, and not hard at all!"

"Just listen to him talk!" Nyurka cried.

"Girls, I've got something real wonderful to tell you," the girl with the hoarse voice exclaimed joyfully. "I know of a bush growing not far from here that glows at night right up till dawn with the most beautiful blue fire. But I'm afraid to go near it."

"What makes it glow like that, Klava?" asked Nyurka in a frightened voice.

"'Cause there's a magic gold pencil buried in the ground under the bush. Once you get that pencil you can wish anything and it will come true!"

"Give it me!" the little boy whined.

"Give you what?"

"The gold pencil!"

"Leave me alone!"

"Give it me!" the little boy repeated and began to sob loudly. "Give me the pencil, you bad girl."

"So that's how you behave!" Nyurka cried giving him a hard ringing slap. "You'll be the death of me! Why, oh why had I brought you into the world!"

Strangely these words at once had a quieting effect on the youngster.

"Oh my dear," began Klava in feigned sweet tones. "Children need not be spanked ever. They need to be taught. Teach them things as I do so they won't grow up good-for-nothings but will be helpful to themselves and to others."

"But what shall I teach them when they don't want to learn anything," retorted Nyurka heatedly.

"They will if you'll teach them things," Klava argued. "Teach them all you know. Look at the kid here, he's been whimpering instead of looking at the hosts of flowers all around and learning their names."

In a minute Klava was asking the youngster the names of the flowers that grew in the meadow. When she discovered that he was ignorant of most of the names but was eager to learn she proceeded to teach them to him, making him repeat each new word several times. It was like a game and the boy was quite fascinated.

I listened, greatly amazed by the girl's knowledge; she knew the names of practically all the flowers and herbs that grew in the field. This lesson in botany was unexpectedly interrupted by a sudden shriek let out by the little boy.

"I've cut myself. Why did you bring me here right into the prickles, you bad girls. How will I get home now?"

"For shame, girls, why do you hurt the little boy?" came the cracked voice of an old man.

"We've done nothing to him, Grandpa Pakhom," said Klava. "You're always getting others into trouble," she added in an undertone to the boy.

I could hear the old man approaching the group of children. Then he looked down into the lake and, catching sight of my fishing rod, said: "Here's a man trying to catch fish and look at the row you're making. As if the meadow is not big enough for you all."

"Where's he fishing, I want to fish, too!" the little boy cried.

"Don't you dare climb down, you idiot, you'll fall into the water," Nyurka screamed.

The children soon went away without my having seen them. But the old man walked down to the edge of the bank and coughed. "Can you spare me a cigarette?" he asked with some hesitation.

I offered him one and to get it he clambered down the steep bank, stumbling, swearing, and clutching at tangles of bramble. He was a frail, shrunken old man and in his hand he held a huge knife in a leather sheath.

"I've come to cut the twigs," he explained, evidently thinking I may be suspicious about the knife. "I do a little weaving, baskets, fishing-tackle and such things."

I told him of my admiration for the little village girl who knew the name of all the flowers and grasses so well.

"Oh you mean Klava?" he said. "She's the daughter of the stableman at the collective-farm. And she's got a grandmother who knows more about herbs than anybody for miles and miles round. You should talk to *her* about flowers. Yes," he added after pausing with a sigh, "each flower has a name, a sort of passport."

After I offered him another cigarette he went away and I followed.

As I emerged from the tangle of bushes on to the road by the meadow I caught sight of the three girls whose talk I had overheard far ahead of me. They were carrying big bunches of flowers and one of them was dragging the little boy who wore a huge cap by the hand. The children walked fast, the heels of their bare feet flashing in the distance. Across the Oka, beyond Yesenino, spread the ruddy glow which the slanting rays of the setting sun lent to the wall of forest stretching eastward.

VOCABULARY NOTES

or a long time I kept turning over in my mind the idea of compiling a number of dictionaries of a special character and actually began working on them and collecting material.

There could be one dictionary, I thought, devoted solely to words relating to nature, another of interesting dialect words, a third of words used by people of different professions, and a fourth of slang, officious words, vulgarisms, obsolete words, unnecessary borrowings from foreign languages, all that must be weeded out of Russian speech. This last as a guide to those inclined to be careless and inaccurate in the use of words.

The idea of compiling a dictionary of nature words occurred to me on the day I was fishing in the lake and had overheard the little farm girl name every flower and herb that grew in the meadow. My plan was, in addition to definitions, to have passages from literature to illustrate the meanings of the words. For example, beside the word "icicle" it would be appropriate to reproduce the following passage from Prishvin:

"The long, thickly grown roots of trees jutting from dark caves in the sheer river-bank had turned into icicles which grew longer and longer and now almost reached into the water. When the gentle spring breeze ruffled the water's surface and the small waves touched the dangling icicles, they swayed and jingled and that jingling was spring's first music, sweet as the strains of Aeolian harp."

To make the word "September" come alive in the imagination I would quote the following lines from Baratynsky:

And here's September! Tarrying its dawn,
The sun gleams with a brilliance cold,
And mirrored in the rippling pond
A sunbeam trembles, dimly gold.

I thought a good deal about how these various dictionaries should be compiled, particularly the dictionary of nature words. The latter could be classified into categories, such as forests, meadows, fields, seasons, meteorological phenomena, water, rivers and lakes, plants and animals. A dictionary of this type I knew must be compiled in such a way as to be as readable as a work of fiction. Only then would it do justice to the nature of our land and the richness of our language.

The immensity of such a task was obvious. One person couldn't do it. A lifetime would not be enough for it. Yet every time I thought of this dictionary I longed to be twenty years younger to be able to undertake at least part of the work.

I began making notes. Later I lost them, and now it is extremely difficult to reconstruct them from memory. I spent one summer collecting flowers and herbs, studying their names and properties with the help of an old book on plants. I found it a most fascinating occupation. I wondered at the perfection of nature's processes, revealed to me in every petal, blossom, root and seed I studied.

In one strange experience I had I actually *felt* the wisdom of Nature's ways. This happened one autumn while I was on a fishing trip with a friend. We fished in a deep long lake which many centuries back had been an old bed of the Oka, but had long ago broken away from the river. The lake was surrounded by thickets so dense that to reach the water was extremely difficult and in some places impossible. A good many prickly seeds of burdock and other plants stuck to the sweater I wore when fishing.

The first two days were clear but cold and we slept in a tent without undressing. On the third day it rained. My sweater was quite damp when I had gone to sleep. In the middle of the night I felt a strange pricking in my chest and arms as if by pins. I soon discovered that I was being pricked by the round flat seeds of some grass that had stuck to my sweater. They had absorbed the moisture in my clothes, had begun to move in spirals and were piercing through the sweater and getting at my bare skin.

I never stop wondering at Nature's clever ways. A seed falls to the ground and lies there motionless waiting for the first rainfall. There is no sense in the seed making its way into the soil while it is dry. But as soon as it gets moist that seed twists into a spiral, swells, begins to live, pushes into the ground and grows.

This has been a digression. Yet writing about seeds called to my mind another thing that I have found fascinating in nature and which to me is in a way symbolic of the fate of books. I mean the strange way in which the sweet scent of the lime, a romantic tree which grows in our parks, can be savoured only at a distance, as though the tree were encircled by its own fragrance. I don't know Nature's reason for this, but I can't help thinking that literature worthy of the name is like lime-blossoms. It requires distance, or rather the test of time, for it to be rightly appraised and for its true powers, its degree of perfection, its message and its beauty to be fully appreciated.

Time can do many things; it can extinguish love and other emotions and erase our memories of men. But it is powerless against genuine literature. Saltykov-Shchedrin said that literature was not subject to the law of death. Pushkin wrote: "My soul in the melodious music of the lyre will my remains outlive and death outwit." And in one of Fet's poems we read: "This leaf that's dried and dropped will in gleaming gold live forever in a song."

Similar thoughts have been voiced over and over again by writers, poets, artists and scholars of all ages and nations. And they should imbue those of us who are writers with a sense of great responsibility for our art. They should make us conscious of the great gulf that separates literature in the true sense of the word from the dull, inferior rubbish that often goes under that name and that is capable only of maiming and degrading the human spirit.

It is a far cry from the scent of lime-blossoms to thoughts on the immortality of literature. Yet it is in the nature of the human mind to follow a train of associations. Will not a tiny pea, or perhaps the neck of a broken bottle, set the teller of tales off on his story?

Still, I shall try to remember some of the notes I made for the dictionaries I hoped to see published one day. Some of our writers, as far as I know, have their own "private" vocabularies. But they do not show these to anybody and speak of them rarely and reluctantly.

What I have already discussed in relation to a number of Russian words has also been partly reconstructed from my "dictionary notes."

The first notes I made were of words connected with the forest. Born and bred in the south, where there are practically no forests at all, it was natural that in Central Russia I should be more attracted to the woodlands than to anything else in the landscape. One of the first words I put down was *глухомань* glookhoman* a word I first heard used among forest rangers. It is not in the dictionary and means approximately "the denseness of the forest." To my mind it at once brings a picture of dense, slumbering mossy forests, damp thickets, branches broken by the wind, the smell of mouldering plants and decayed tree-trunks, greenish twilight and deep silence. Then followed the more common words pertaining to the forest, simple words, yet each helping to conjure up a most beautiful picture of various kinds of forests and trees.

But to appreciate these words one must truly love the forest. And if you do, even so dry and technical a term as "the forest boundary pole" will at once bring to your mind a pleasing picture. Around each of these poles, cutting across narrow clearings, is a little mound of sand from the pit that was dug for it and it is overgrown with tall grass and strawberries. These sunlit poles on which butterflies with folded wings warm themselves and creeping ants go gravely about their business, tempt you to rest awhile after a long tramp. It is warmer by these poles than in the woods (or perhaps it only seems so). You drop to the ground, leaning your back against the pole, listening to the rustling of the crowns of the trees and gazing up into the clear blue sky with silver-fringed white clouds sailing across it. These clearings are so deserted that I imagine you could spend a month there without seeing a single soul. In the sky and clouds there is the same noonday peace as in the woods, as in the dry little

* The "kh" is pronounced like the "ch" in the word *loch.—Tr.*

cup of the bluebell, dipping down to the ground, and as there is deep in the heart.

Sometimes you recognize a pole that is an old friend of yours of a year or two ago. And each time you think of how much water had passed under the bridges since your last encounter; the places you have visited, the sorrows and joys you have experienced, while the pole had been standing in the very same spot where you had left it, day and night, summer and winter, waiting for you like a true friend. Only now it is more thickly covered with yellow lichen and entwined by dodder right up to its top. The dodder, budding and basking in the woodland warmth, has the pungent smell of almonds.

It is from the top of a fire watch-tower that a particularly good view of the forest opens—the vistas stretching to the horizon, rising up hills and descending to glens, the serrated walls of trees, enclosing sand-pits, here and there the silvery sheen of a forest lake or ruddy pool coming into sight. The forest seems boundless, unexplored, its mysterious depths beckoning with a force that it is impossible to resist. And when I feel the call of the woods I lose no time in shouldering a knapsack, taking a compass and plunging deep into that green sylvan ocean.

Arkady Gaidar and I were once drawn into the woods in this way. We roamed through a trackless forest all day and all night, and the stars peeping between the tall pine-tops seemed to be shining for us alone. Just before dawn we emerged by a meandering stream over which a warm mist had settled. After lighting a fire at the water's edge, we sat by the stream in silence for a long time, listening to the rippling of the water under a snag and to the sad cry of the elk. We sat thus smoking till a delicate blue spread over the eastern sky.

"A hundred years of a life like this!" exclaimed Gaidar. "What do you say?"

"Even more! But it wouldn't be a bad idea to have some tea. Give me the kettle."

He made his way in the dark to the stream and I heard him scrub the kettle with some sand, and swear when the wire handle broke off. A minute later he was singing a song which ran like this:

> *Forests deep, woods with outlaws rife,*
> *Dark—since times long ago.*
> *Glinting steel of the hidden knife,*
> *Whetted—for a cruel blow...*

His singing had a strangely soothing effect. The silent forest too seemed to be listening to it, only the brook kept up its babble, fretting at the snag that blocked its way.

Russian words pertaining to the seasons of the year are extremely expressive and numerous, bringing to us the full charm of Nature in her changing garb.

There are ever so many words relating to mists, winds, clouds and expanses of water. Russian is particularly rich in words that have to do with rivers. Among the people I have knocked about are several ferrymen and I often wondered at the picturesqueness of their speech. Crowds crossing the river on a raft or ferry-boat are generally gay, colourful and noisy. There is a constant hum of talk and a brisk exchange of repartee. Wives as they leisurely handle the mooring ropes tease their husbands. Long-haired, sleek-looking ponies munch at the hay in the carts being carried across the river, chewing it hurriedly and casting sidelong glances at lorries in which bagged sucking pigs going to the slaughter kick and squeal. The menfolk can be seen enjoying their home-made cigarettes of green, bitter shag, smoking them down to small butts and burning their fingertips.

And you—you sit on some hay spread over the raft with its loosely joined logs, smoke and listen to the conversation around you, the latest farm news, and bits of general news, some strange tales and here and there pearls of wisdom.

As for the ferrymen, they, for the most part, have seen a great deal of life. They are sharp-tongued and talkative, particularly ready for a chat in the evening when there are no more crowds to be ferried across the river. Their day's work is done when the sun sets gently behind the steep river-banks, and the mosquitoes fill the air with their buzzing. They take a cigarette from you which they hold between rope-roughened fingers, and say that light tobacco is only for gentlemen and not good for tough throats like theirs. Nevertheless they smoke the cigarette with relish and, squinting at the river, set the ball of conversation rolling.

On the whole, the river-bank and the moorages, with their bustling, motley crowds and their peculiar traditions and customs, afford excellent opportunities for the study of language. In this respect the Volga and Oka are particularly interesting. These two rivers are as much part of Russian life and tradition as are Moscow, the Kremlin, Pushkin, Tolstoi, Chaikovsky, Chaliapin, the statue of the Bronze Horseman in Leningrad and the Tretyakov Art Gallery in Moscow.

There is a beautiful poem containing descriptions of the Volga and particularly the Oka by the poet Yazykov, whose language Pushkin greatly admired. Here are a few lines from it:

> *... so rich in woods, so overflowing,*
> *The sandy soil unhindering its course,*
> *It flows in splendour, majesty and glory,*
> *Protected by its venerable shores.*

There are many local dialect words in Russian. Too free and indiscriminate use of these words in dialogue is a fault common among inexperienced and immature writers. Words, chosen at random to give "local atmosphere," are often entirely unfamiliar to the general reader and only annoy him.

The height to which we must aspire is accurate use of the Russian literary language, a language which is extremely flexible. It may be enriched by local words provided this is done with great discretion, for along with extremely colourful and apt local words, there are many that are vulgar and jar on the ear. Also, when the writer introduces local words, it is necessary that their meaning (if they are entirely unfamiliar to the reader) should be clear at once from the context.

Literature that is confusing, affected, and unnecessarily startling in its use of words, has no appeal whatever for the majority of our readers. The clearer the atmosphere, the brighter the sunlight, and so with prose, the more lucid it is, the more perfect will its style be, and the stronger will it appeal to the reader. "Simplicity is one of beauty's essentials," said Tolstoi.

Meeting and talking to peasants has helped me to enrich my own language. There was an old peasant I met in a little village in the Ryazan Region. Semyon Vasilyevich Yelesin, or Grandad Semyon, as he was affectionately called, had the innocent soul of a child. He was a hardworking man, content to lead a very simple life, a typical Russian peasant—proud, noble-hearted, generous.

I greatly enjoyed hearing him talk, for he had the most original and picturesque way of expressing himself. It was his secret hope to become a carpenter and be "a real craftsman." But he died before he could realize his ambition. A man's personality lends charm to his surroundings. So when Grandad Semyon died in the winter of 1954 the neighbourhood lost a good deal of its attraction for me and I couldn't bring myself to make another trip to that part of the country and go to the sand-swept little mound by the river where the old man's remains lie.

The writer's desire to increase his stock of words should know no bounds. My own experiences along these lines have been devious and varied. Once, for example, I made a special study of nautical terms. One of my sources were books containing sailing instructions for captains. I found these extremely fascinating. Here one could learn everything there was to know about the sea—its fathomless depths, currents, winds, ports, lighthouses, submerged mountain ridges, shoals. I learned what it was that contributed to smooth sailing at sea and many other things.

The first log-book that fell into my hands dealt with sailing along the Black and Azov seas. I was amazed at the beauty and accuracy of its language. But there was something strange about the phrases which at first puzzled me. I soon realized that this strangeness was due to the mingling of expressions long obsolete with quite modern words and terms. It appeared that these books, first published at the beginning of the 19th century, came out regularly at set intervals, each new edition replenished by fresh entries in a more modern language, while the old part of the book remained unaltered. Thus these books were interesting material for one who wished to trace the changes that words and their meanings undergo with time.

The language used by seafarers is vital, refreshing and replete with humour, a language well worth studying.

INCIDENT AT "ALSHWANG STORES"

he trying winter of 1921, a year of Civil War and famine, found me in Odessa. I was living in what had been the second-floor fitting rooms of the former "Alshwang Stores," which sold ready-made clothes.

I had three rooms with long wall mirrors which both the poet Eduard Bagritsky and I tried very hard to detach from the walls so that we could barter them for something to eat at the market. But of no avail. After all our drastic handling not one of the mirrors was even cracked.

There was no furniture in the rooms, except for three cases with mouldy shavings. Fortunately the glass door could easily be removed from its hinges. Every night I took it off and placed it on two of the cases and made a bed for myself—and a slippery bed it was too.

I would wake up several times in the night because the old thing I used for a mattress kept sliding to the floor under me. As soon as the mattress started slipping down I would open my eyes and lie as still as possible, afraid to make the slightest movement, foolishly hoping that in that way I may induce the mattress to stop playing tricks. But it kept slipping slowly but surely, quite scornful of my stratagem.

This may seem funny now, but it wasn't then, with a violent northeastern wind blowing from the frozen sea and sweeping along the granite pavements. It had not snowed once and that made the frost even more biting.

In the former fitting room there stood the universal "bourzhuika" of the Civil War times—a very inadequate stove made of tin. But there was no firewood. Even had there been any, it would have been useless to try to heat three huge rooms with that poor makeshift of a stove. I only used it for boiling "carrot tea," for which purpose a few old newspapers sufficed.

My third case served as a desk. In the evening, wrapped up in all the warm clothes I possessed, I would read Georgy Shengeli's translations of José Maria Heredia's poems by the light of a little wick floating in oil. These poems were published in Odessa in that grim year of famine, and I must say they helped to keep up our spirits. We felt as staunch as the Romans and would repeat a line written by Shengeli himself which ran something like this: "Friends, we are Romans, we are being bled white."

We were not being bled white, by any means, but we were young and full of the joy of living, and we found the cold and hunger trying at times. But we never grumbled.

The ground-floor of the "Alshwang Stores" was occupied by an Arts and Crafts Co-operative, a bustling, somewhat suspicious outfit managed by a grumpy, elderly artist known in Odessa as the "Ad King." This co-operative took orders for signs, ladies' fancy hats, wooden sandals (in "Greek style" with wooden soles and a few leather straps), and for film posters, done in glue paint on crooked bits of plywood. One day the co-operative had a piece of good fortune: an order for a figurehead for the steamer *Pestel*, which was to go on its first voyage to Batum. It was the only vessel the Black Sea could boast of in those days. The figurehead was made from sheet iron with a gold floral ornament painted on a black background. Everyone helped with the work, even Zhora Kozlovsky, the militiaman, came off his beat to look in now and then.

At that time I was managing editor of *The Seaman*, a local newspaper. There were many young writers on its staff, among them Valentin Katayev, Eduard Bagritsky, Babel, Yuri Olesha and Ilya Ilf. Among the older and more experienced writers, Andrei Sobol, kind, restless and always excited about something, was a frequent visitor at the office. He once brought us a short story, disorderly and all mixed up, but undoubtedly a work of talent and dealing with an interesting subject.

We all read it and it put us in an awkward position. To print it in the sloppy way it was written was impossible. Yet no one had the courage to suggest to Sobol that he rewrite it—something he could never be persuaded to do. This was not because it would hurt his vanity (as a matter of fact Sobol had no vanity at all) but because, being temperamental and high-strung, no sooner was he done with a piece of work, than he lost all interest in it.

What to do with the manuscript was something that worried us all. With us was our proof-reader, Blagov, an elderly person, the ex-managing director of *Russkoye Slovo*, one of tsarist Russia's most widely read newspapers, and formerly the right-hand man of Sytin, the well-known publisher.

Blagov, quiet, and somewhat self-conscious about his past, was so staid and respectable-looking that he contrasted strangely with the host of bedraggled, boisterous young people filling our office.

I took Sobol's manuscript home with me for a second reading. At about ten o'clock that night Zhora Kozlovsky, the militiaman, knocked on the front door. It was pitch black in the town, the streets were deserted with only the wind howling fiercely, particularly at the crossroads. After twisting a newspaper into a long thick band and lighting it, I went to open the massive front door, bolted by a rusty length of gas-pipe. It was no use taking my makeshift lamp; even staring at it was enough to put it out, let alone the least movement of air. I had but to fix my gaze on it when it would at once begin to crackle plaintively, flicker and slowly die. That is why I even avoided looking at it.

"A person here to see you," said Zhora, the militiaman. "But don't you think I'm going to let him in without your vouching for his identity. Remember, the shop on the ground floor's got three hundred billion rubles' worth of paints alone."

Considering that my salary at the newspaper came to a billion a month (at market prices I could buy no more than 40 boxes of matches with it), the sum Zhora mentioned was not at all as fabulous as might be imagined.

Blagov was at the door. After I told Zhora who he was, he let him pass, promising in two hours to drop in to warm up and drink a cup of hot water.

"I've been thinking about that story by Sobol," said Blagov. "It's a talented piece of writing. Something should be done about it. I'm an old hand at the newspaper game, as you know, and I wouldn't like to see a good story slip out of our hands."

"What do you suggest?"

"Let me have the manuscript. I swear I won't change a single word in it. I'll have to stay in your rooms because being out at such a late hour is risky. I'll go over the manuscript in your presence."

" 'Go over'—that means you're going to edit it?" I asked.

"I've already told you what I intend to do, I shan't delete a single word, nor shall I add anything."

"Then what are you going to do?"

"You'll see."

I was puzzled. Here was Blagov, calm and stolid as ever, and yet he brought an air of mystery into my rooms. I was intrigued and agreed to give him a free hand.

He drew out of his pocket the stub of an unusually thick, gold-striped candle, lit it, put it down on the case which served as a desk, sat down on my worn-out valise and with a flat carpenter's pencil bent over the manuscript.

At about midnight Zhora Kozlovsky dropped in. I had just boiled some water and was brewing our "tea"—this time thinly sliced roasted beets instead of the usual strips of dried carrots.

"I'll have you know," began Zhora, "that from the street you look like a pair of bloody counterfeiters. What's your game anyway?"

"We're just fixing up a story for our next issue," I replied.

"Well, I'll have you know," Zhora repeated, "that any other militiaman would have checked up on you. So you'd better thank God—of course, there is no God—that I'm on the beat and you've got to do with me, a lover of culture, and not just any plain bobby. As for counterfeiters, I can tell you there are some real sharks at that game. They'll take a hunk of manure and make dollars out of it and a passport into the bargain. I heard tell that they have a marble cast of a hand of remarkable beauty lying on black velvet cushion in the Louvre, in Paris. Whose hand do you think it is? Sarah Bernhardt's? Chopin's? Vera Kholodnaya's? You've guessed wrong. It's the

121

hand of Europe's most notorious forger, his name's slipped my mind. They cut his head off but kept his hand, as though he were a violin virtuoso. Well, what do you think of that?"

"Not much," I replied. "Have you any saccharine to spare?"

"Yes," replied Zhora, "in pills. I'll let you have some."

It was morning when Blagov finished working on the story and he wouldn't show it to me till it was typed out at the office.

When I finished reading the story I gasped. It was in crystal-clear and smooth prose, vivid and lucid. Not a shade left of the old crammedness and tortuous circumlocution. And, what was more, not a single word had been deleted or added to the manuscript.

I looked at Blagov. He was smoking a fat cigarette of a Kuban blend of tobacco as black as tea and grinning.

"Why, that's a miracle!" I cried. "How did you do it?"

"All I did was put the punctuation marks in the right place. Sobol's punctuation is atrocious. And then I changed the periods and paragraphing. That made all the difference. Pushkin spoke of the importance of punctuation, you know. Punctuation marks are like music symbols. They are there for cohesion, for getting the correct balance between different parts of the sentence."

The next day when the story appeared, Andrei Sobol swept into the office hatless, as was his custom, his hair dishevelled and a fire in his eyes that was hard to fathom.

"Who touched my story?" he boomed. Swinging his stick in the air, he brought it down with a bang on a desk littered with files of newspapers from which clouds of dust at once rose up.

"Nobody touched it," I replied. "If you like you can check it with the original."

"It's a lie, a damn lie," retorted Sobol. "I'll find out who it was."

A storm was brewing; our more timid comrades began quickly to retire from the room. And as usual the voices attracted our two typists who rushed in tapping with their wooden sandals.

"I touched your story," began Blagov in a quiet matter-of-fact voice, "if by 'touching' you mean putting the punctuation marks where they belong. Besides, as the paper's proof-reader, I was only doing my duty."

Hearing this, Sobol dashed up to Blagov, seized both his hands and shook them heartily. A minute later he was hugging Blagov and kissing him three times in the Moscow fashion.

"Thanks," he said, very much agitated. "Thanks for the lesson you have taught me—a little too late in the day, I'm afraid. I feel like a criminal when I think how I used to mutilate my writings."

In the evening Sobol, who had somehow managed to get hold of a half-bottle of cognac, came to my rooms. Blagov, Eduard Bagritsky, and Zhora Kozlovsky, when relieved from his beat, were there too and we had quite a celebration, drinking to the glory of literature in general and punctuation marks in particular.

We all agreed that a full stop in the right place may work wonders.

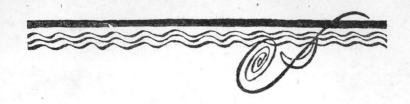

SOME SIDELIGHTS ON
WRITING

 ost writers have their own particular geniuses to inspire them. Generally these geniuses are writers too.

Read a few lines by your particular genius and you at once feel the urge to write yourself. You are intoxicated, infected by the germ to write and you can't help taking up your pen at once. But a surprising thing that I have noticed is that these geniuses are generally poles apart in temperament, manner of writing, and subject-matter from the writers they influence.

I know a writer, a hardened realist, writing about life's commonplaces, a sober-minded and even-tempered person, who draws inspiration from Alexander Green, one of our greatest literary dreamers.

Gaidar used to say that nobody inspired him as much as Dickens. As to myself, I always feel the urge to write after reading Stendhal's *Letters from Rome*, and I am amazed at the difference between my thoughts and style and those of Stendhal. One autumn, after reading Stendhal,

I wrote "Cordon 273" about forest reservations along the Pra River. There is absolutely nothing in the story to suggest Stendhal.

I have not thought of an explanation in this particular case. Yet I imagine there must be one. I have mentioned this instance merely as an excuse for discussing some of the working habits and practices of certain writers.

There was, for example, Pushkin's great preference for writing in autumn, so that his "Boldino Autumn" has become a synonym for fruitful and prolific writing.

"Autumn is approaching," Pushkin wrote to one of his friends. "It is my favourite season. I am at my best and more than ever fit to write."

Perhaps it is not so difficult to account for autumn's stimulating effect, particularly late autumn. Autumn is crystalline and bracing with a poignant, fading beauty, with clear vistas and limpid breath. Autumn imparts a severity to nature's patterns. In autumn as the woods hourly shed their russet gold, leaving the trees and boughs bare, everything is brought into sharper relief. Clear effects are the keynote to autumn's landscape. They are modulated into one dominant tone which takes possession of the writer's soul, imagination and heart. Sprays, cool and clear, with a tinkling of ice come from the fountain of prose or poetry—one's head is clear when one writes, the heart-beats reverberate, only the fingers are slightly chilled.

In autumn men's thoughts grow mellow. "And the precious harvest's ripe, in grains your thoughts you gather, and further the fullness of the destinies of men," wrote Bagritsky.

Pushkin, as he himself used to say, felt younger with every autumn. Autumn rejuvenated him. Evidently Goethe was right when he said that geniuses were blessed with more than one youth.

It was in autumn that Pushkin wrote an amazingly beautiful poem dealing with the creative process of writing.

> And I forget the world—and in the silence deep
> I'm sweetly lulled to sleep by my imagination.
> And poesy awakens now within me:
> My soul is stirred with lyrical elation,
> I hear its tremulous voice, it strives as though in
> > sleep
> To give itself at last complete and free expression—
> And then my phantom guests come to me in a stream,
> They are my friends of old, the children of my dream.
> And thoughts to valour roused my mind engage,
> And simple rhymes come hastening towards them,
> My fingers seek a pen, the pen gropes for a page,
> A minute—and the verse will flow unstemmed....

It is interesting to note that Pushkin never stopped to polish up lines with which he had difficulty, but went on writing, waiting for moments of inspiration to return to the unfinished bits.

I watched Arkady Gaidar at work and found his writing habits strikingly different from those of any other writer I knew.

We lived at the time in a village in the Meshchora woods, Gaidar in a spacious cottage overlooking the village street and I in what had once been the bathhouse in the back garden of the same house. Gaidar was writing his *Fate of a Drummer*, and we agreed that we would work from morning till lunch without a break and would on no account disturb each other.

But in the morning as I settled down to work in front of the open window and had not written more than a quarter of a page Arkady appeared and walked by my window. I pretended not to notice him. He walked away muttering something to himself but soon was back again passing outside my window—this time whistling and feigning a cough so that I could see that he wanted to attract my attention. I kept silent. Then he passed by my window for the third time and looked at me with irritation. But I did not open my mouth.

"Listen," he said losing his patience. "Stop playing the fool. Why, if I could write at the rate you do, I wouldn't grudge my friends a few minutes of my time, and my complete works would run to no less than one hundred and eighteen volumes."

He evidently liked this figure.

"One hundred and eighteen volumes! No less!" he repeated with satisfaction.

"All right," I said. "What is it you want?"

"Just for you to listen to a marvellous sentence I've got in my head."

"Out with it, then!"

"Well, hear it: ' "He's suffered, the old man's truly suffered," said the passengers.' It is good?"

"How do I know? It depends where it stands and what it refers to."

" 'What it refers to,' " he aped me. "It refers to what it should refer and stands where it should stand. To hell with you—you can go on polishing up your muck, while I put down that sentence."

But he was not gone long. In twenty minutes he was back, again pacing up and down outside my window.

"Have you thought up another brilliant sentence?" I asked.

"I always suspected you were a dirty high-brow, now I'm certain of it."

"Very well, I wish you would stop disturbing me then."

"Yes, too damn stuck-up, that's what you are!" And with this retort he went away.

In five minutes he was back, yelling a new sentence at me from the distance. It did not sound bad, and I told him so. This changed his whole attitude.

"Now you're talking," he said. "I won't disturb you any more! I'll manage without your precious opinion."

And unexpectedly he broke into the most abominable French, a language he was studying at the time with great enthusiasm.

"Au revoir, monsieur, l'ecrivain Russe-Sovietique!" he shouted at me.

He returned to the garden several times after that but never came near my window, pacing along one of the paths and muttering to himself.

Such was his way of writing. He would think up bits of his story while walking and then rush into the house to put them down, so that his day was divided between walking in the garden and writing in the house. This made it difficult to imagine that Gaidar was getting on with his story. But he was. In fact he soon finished *The Fate of a Drummer*, and in the best of spirits walked in to tell me so.

"Want me to read the thing to you?"

Of course, I wanted nothing better.

"Well then get ready to listen," said Gaidar, and with his hands in his pockets took up an attitude in the centre of the room.

"But where's the manuscript?" I asked.

"Only fourth-rate conductors need to have the score in front of them," Gaidar declared sententiously. "What do I want with the manuscript? It is peacefully resting on my desk. Well, shall I begin?"

And he rattled off the story he had written by heart from the first to the last line.

"Yet, I can't take your word for it, I'm sure you must have missed a thing here and there," I said.

"I'll bet you I haven't! We'll allow no more than ten slips for the whole story. And if you lose you go down to Ryazan tomorrow and buy that nice ancient barometer we saw an old woman selling at the market. Remember her, she put a lamp-shade over her head when it began to rain. Now I'll go and fetch the manuscript."

When he recited the story a second time I had my eyes on the manuscript. Indeed he made no more than a few unimportant slips. We argued for several days about who won the bet and it all ended to Arkady's great delight in my buying the barometer. The barometer was a huge brass thing and we thought it would be a good guide in our fishing outings. But it let us down the very first time we used it showing "fair weather" when it rained for three days and we got drenched to the skin.

With what pleasure I recall those "good old times" spent in jesting, playing practical jokes on each other, arguing about literature and going fishing! Somehow it was all wonderfully conducive to writing.

I happened to be with Konstantin Fedin when he began writing his novel *No Ordinary Summer*. I earnestly hope that Konstantin Fedin will forgive me for the liberty I take in describing him at work on his novel. But a description of the manner of writing of any writer, and particularly a master of prose like Fedin, is of interest and benefit to writers as well as to all lovers of literature.

We were staying in Gagri, in the Caucasus, in a small house at the very margin of the sea. The house, which had the air of cheap pre-revolutionary furnished rooms, was a tumble-down, rickety affair. When a sto m rose and the waves beat violently against the shore, .t shook and rattled and creaked in the wind, ready to break up before our very eyes. Doors kept opening and shutting, sometimes with such force that the plaster fell off the ceilings.

On stormy nights all the stray dogs of the neighbourhood took refuge on and beneath the cottage terrace. Now and then, when nobody was in, they would slink inside, and we would find them peacefully snoring in our beds.

For this reason when we entered the house we were always on guard, ready for an emergency if the dogs were fierce. Timid dogs were different, they would jump off the bed at once and dash out with a piercing yelp. Yet they, too, were liable sometimes out of sheer fear to snap at our legs on their way out. But a cur of the insolent, worldly-wise kind was not likely even to stir. It would watch us with flashing eyes and snarl so angrily that there was no alternative but to call in the neighbours.

The window of Fedin's room overlooked the terrace facing the sea. In stormy weather the wicker chairs would be heaped up in front of his window to protect them from splashes. And there would be a pack of hounds sitting on top of them and staring through the window at Fedin who sat writing at his desk. The dogs whined ruefully, longing to be admitted into the warm, bright room.

At first Fedin complained that the sight of the brutes made him shudder. It was indeed terrible to look up from one's writing and meet the glare of a score of canine eyes, all flashing with hatred. They made Fedin feel extremely uncomfortable, perhaps even slightly guilty that he was sitting in a warm cheerful room, engaged in so senseless a business as passing pen over paper. However, in a short time he got used to the dogs.

Most writers work mornings, some in the daytime and very few at night.

Fedin had a marvellous capacity for working, if he wished, all day and most of the night. He would say that the roar of the sea helped him to write at night. The silence, on the other hand, made him restless and he could not concentrate.

"The sea is quiet, come out on the terrace and let's listen," he said waking me up in the night.

The night was indeed wrapped in a deep tranquillity. We listened, trying to catch the faintest sound of a splash, but could hear nothing except the ringing in our ears and the throb of our coursing blood. High overhead the dim light of stars pricked the universal darkness. We were so accustomed to the roar of the sea that the silence was rather oppressive and Fedin could not take up his pen that night.

Fedin was not writing his splendid novel in his usual surroundings. There was something about the whole atmosphere—we were in fact roughing it—that was reminiscent of our young days and was stimulating. Those were the days when a window-sill was just as good as a desk, a wick floating in oil did for a lamp and it was so cold in our unheated rooms that the ink froze in the ink-wells.

By observing Konstantin Fedin at work I learned that he always had a clear picture of what he was going to write before picking up his pen. He never began a new chapter before the chain of events, the thoughts, the development of the characters, were definitely shaped in his mind and he saw exactly how they would fit in into the whole scheme of his work. He hated any looseness in the plot, any slipshod or hazy delineation of character. Prose, he claimed, must be clad in the granite of integrity and harmony.

Flaubert, it will be remembered, spent his whole life in a tortuous search for perfection of style. In his longing for flawlessness of language he went perhaps a little too far. Polishing up and re-writing had become almost a disease with him. At times he would lose faith in his own judgement, grow desperate and end up by emasculating his beautiful writing.

Fedin has been able to strike the golden mean in his writing. The critic in him is always alive, but the critic does not get the upper hand over the writer.

To return to Flaubert—he possessed to a remarkable degree the power of putting himself in the flesh of his characters and living over himself their experiences and sufferings.

When he was writing the scene in which Emma Bovary poisons herself, he himself experienced all the symptoms of poisoning so much so that he required a doctor's attention.

Flaubert always reproached himself for the slowness with which he wrote. He lived in Croisset on the banks of the Seine, near Rouen. The windows of his study, which contained many curios, overlooked the river. In the study a lamp with a green shade burned all night long, extinguished only at daybreak. It is said that Flaubert's windows, particularly on dark nights, served as beacon lights to the fishermen on the Seine and even to the captains of sea-going ships coming up the river from Havre to Rouen. These captains said they had "Monsieur Flaubert's windows" to keep them on course in that section of the river.

Now and then they caught sight of a stockily built man in a brightly patterned oriental dressing-gown, standing at one of the windows with his forehead pressed against the pane, gazing at the Seine with the look of one who was greatly fatigued. But little did the seamen imagine that there stood one of France's greatest writers, wearied by an unflagging struggle for perfect prose, that "accursed liquidy stuff which would not mould into the necessary form."

To Balzac his characters were as much alive as any of the people with whom he was on intimate terms in everyday life. When he thought they were behaving foolishly he would grow livid with anger and call them fools or scoundrels. At other times he would chuckle, pat them on the shoulder approvingly, or console them awkwardly in their grief.

Balzac's belief in the flesh-and-blood existence of his characters and in the indisputability of what he wrote about them bordered on the fantastic. There is even the story—or is it a legend?—of how he had driven a young and innocent nun to a life of sin because she had accidentally been identified with a character in one of his writings.

The little nun whom Balzac describes in his story is sent by her Mother Superior on some errand to Paris and is dazzled by the life she sees there. She spends hours gazing at the gorgeous displays in shop windows. She sees beautiful, perfumed women in exquisite gowns revealing the loveliness of their slender backs, long legs and small pointed breasts—all so suggestive that the women appear almost naked before her eyes.

The atmosphere around her is charged with intoxicating confessions of love, sweet innuendoes and the mad whisperings of men. She is young and beautiful herself and men pursue her in the streets. She hears the same wild utterings and they make her heart flutter. The first kiss wrenched from her by force under the shade of a plane-tree in one of the gardens makes her completely lose her head and cast prudence to the winds. She stays in Paris spending the money in her trust to convert herself into an enchanting Parisienne. A month later she becomes a courtesan.

Balzac in his story used the name of one of the existing convents at the time and the book containing the story fell into the hands of its Mother Superior. In that convent there happened to be a pretty little nun who, in every detail, even in name, answered to the description of Balzac's heroine.

Ordering the little nun to appear before her, the Mother Superior thundered: "Do you know what Monsieur Balzac writes about you? He has tarnished your name and soiled the reputation of our convent. He is a slanderer and a blasphemer. Read this."

The girl read the story and burst into tears.

"You must go immediately to Paris, find Monsieur Balzac, and demand that he clear your name before all France," said the Mother Superior. "If you cannot make him do that, never darken our doors again."

The little nun went to Paris and there with difficulty gained admission to Balzac.

The writer, sitting in a smoke-filled room, his table cluttered with heaps of hurriedly written sheets, was frowning; he hated to be disturbed at his work. Dropping her eyes before his penetrating gaze, the young girl blushed, and praying to God for strength, told the writer what she desired of him. She begged him to remove the slur he had for no reason at all cast on her virginity and piety.

Balzac was puzzled. He could not understand what the pretty shy little nun wanted from him.

"I have cast no slur, everything I write is the sacred truth," he said.

"Monsieur Balzac, have compassion on me. If you refuse to help I do not know what to do."

"What do you mean, you don't know what to do!" cried Balzac jumping to his feet. "You do exactly what I have written in my story. There is no other alternative for you."

"Do you mean to say that I must stay in Paris?" she asked incredulously.

"Yes!" Balzac boomed. "Yes, the deuce take it!"

"And you want me to become...."

"No, the deuce take it!" Balzac boomed again. "I only want you to cast off that ugly black robe and let your young, beautiful body learn what joy and love are. I want you to learn to laugh with delight. Go! go! But not to the streets!"

The nun could not return to the convent because Balzac refused to clear her name. She remained in Paris. A year later she was seen in a students' tavern, in the midst of a crowd of young people, gay, happy and charming.

Writing habits are as varied as the writers themselves.

Among the letters which I had read in the wooden house near Ryazan, addressed to the famous engraver Pozhalostin, were several, as I have already mentioned, from Iordan. In one of these Iordan writes that he had spent two years engraving a copy of an Italian painting, and while working on it had rubbed holes in the brick floor of his studio—a result of the habit he had formed of pacing round the table with his engraver's board.

"I would grow fatigued," wrote Iordan. "Yet I kept walking, moving. And now just think how weary Nikolai Vasilyevich Gogol, used to writing in a standing position at his desk, would get. Here was a true martyr of literature!"

One of Lev Tolstoi's habits was to write in the morning only. He used to say that in each writer lived a critic and the critic was crossest in the morning. At night the critic was asleep and the writer had only his own judgement to fall back on with the result that he wrote a great deal that was poor and superfluous. Tolstoi said, for example, that Jean Jacques Rousseau and Charles Dickens wrote in the morning while Dostoyevsky and Byron, who had formed the habit of writing by night sinned against their own talent.

What affected the quality of Dostoyevsky's writings was, of course, not so much his habit of working nights and drinking tea incessantly as the fact that he was poor and always in debt which compelled him to rush his work.

Pressed for time, he could never take real pains over his writing and give full vent to his literary powers. That is why many of his novels lack the breadth of narrative he could easily have attained in them, and fall short of his own concepts and plans. "Novels are pleasanter in the thinking than in the writing," Dostoyevsky would say.

He tried to prolong the period during which the novel was taking shape in his mind, changing and enhancing the unwritten story. He would keep putting off the time of writing—each day, each hour brought new ideas which, he feared, once the writing was begun, it would be too late to incorporate in the novel.

And that is exactly what would happen. Pressed by debts, he was forced to begin to write before he was really ready for it and many fresh thoughts, images and details came into his mind much too late—when the novel was finished, or as he would say himself, "hopelessly ruined."

"Poverty," Dostoyevsky said, "compels me to hurry and make a business out of writing which invariably has a ruinous effect on my work."

Schiller was able to write only after drinking a half-bottle of champagne and putting his feet into a basin of cold water.

In his youth Chekhov could write on the window-sill in a noisy, overcrowded Moscow flat. He wrote his story "The Huntsman" in the bathhouse. But as the years went by he began to lose this great faculty for facile writing.

Lermontov wrote his verses on anything that was handy, not necessarily paper. And, indeed, they give the impression of being composed on the spur of the moment, first sung in the soul, and then quickly jotted down without subsequent polishing.

Alexei Tolstoi had to have a ream of good-quality paper lying on his desk before he could settle down to write. And he usually began writing a story with nothing but one little detail in his mind. That detail would set him off on a train of events—it was like the unravelling of a magic ball of thread.

As I have already said, he possessed great powers of improvisation, his thoughts running ahead of his words and flowing so fast that he had a hard time keeping up with them. If he ever had to strain himself to write, he ceased writing at once.

That delicious state when a fresh thought or picture rises from the depths of the consciousness and flashes across the mind is familiar to all writers. And if these are not put to paper at once, they may vanish without a trace.

Thoughts and mental pictures have light and movement, but they are as evasive as dreams, the kind of dream the substance of which one remembers after awakening only for a fraction of a second. And no matter how hard one tries to recall the dream afterwards, it is of no avail. All that remains of it is the sensation of having experienced something uncommon, marvellous and delightful.

Hence, the writer must acquire the habit of at once jotting down his thoughts, for the least delay—and they are lost for ever.

It was in cheap cafés that the French poet Béranger wrote his songs. Ilya Ehrenburg, too, as far as I know, found the atmosphere in cafés congenial to writing. Perhaps, there is no better solitude than amidst an animated crowd, if, of course, there are no importunate distractions.

Hans Christian Andersen liked thinking up his fairytales in the woods. He had splendid eyesight and could see every curve and every crack on a bit of bark or on an old pine cone as through a magnifying glass. These were the little things out of which it was so easy to weave a tale.

A moss-covered tree stump, a little ant dragging a midge with green transparent wings on its back, like a gallant robber kidnapping a beautiful princess, were enough to set the writer off on a train of creative thought.

Of my own ways and habits of writing there is not much to tell, except that when I sit down to write I hate to have anything on my mind—such as conferences or public appearances, for example. And apropos of that, I would like to mention that too much of our writers' time is taken up with meetings and public functions. These, of course, are important, but we must remember that to tax writers with too much public activity may mean taking precious time away that could be put to better use—to the expression of talent. Literature, after all, is the writer's chief business.

But it is still worse when there is some real worry or trouble harassing you. Then, I find, it is better not to take up the pen at all, but to wait till your mind is free from all cares. I always write best when I am light-hearted. Only then do I give myself wholly to my work and can take my time over it.

At various periods in my life I had what I consider quite ideal conditions for writing. During one such period I was the only passenger on board a boat sailing in the winter from Batum to Odessa. The sea was grey, cold and calm with the shores shrouded in an ashen-grey mist and the distant mountain ridges wrapped in heavy, leaden clouds, like in a lethargic dream. I wrote in my cabin, now and then getting up, and looking at the shores through the porthole. There was only the throb of the engines and the cries of the sea-gulls to break the silence. I wrote with great ease. There was no one to disturb me, nothing to take my mind off my work. I was wholly dedicated to what I was writing—and this was a great happiness. The open sea protected me from outside intrusion, while the sensation of motion, of wide open spaces, of calls at ports and the vague anticipation of brief non-committal meetings with people—all were conducive to writing. And as the steamer ploughed through the pale, wintry water, I felt ineffably happy—perhaps in the knowledge that my story was going well.

Another occasion on which I wrote with a light heart and the words flowed with ease from my pen was in the attic of a little cottage to the lone crackling of the candle-light. Dark and windless, the September night spread about me, and in the same way as the open sea, protected me from intrusion. The old orchard at the back of the house was shedding its foliage and my heart went out to it like to a human being—a sensation that somehow spurred me to write. Late at night I would go out into the dark to fetch some water from the well to make my tea, and I felt that the clanging of the pail in the well and the sound of human footsteps made it easier for the old orchard to endure the long autumn night. Cold, bare woods stretched for miles and miles round. There, I knew, were woodland lakes which reflected the glimmer of the stars as they had done perhaps on just such a lonely night a thousand years ago.

Above all, I can write well when I have something pleasant to look forward to, even if it is nothing more than the prospect of fishing in some far-off forest stream in the shade of the weeping willow.

ATMOSPHERE AND LITTLE TOUCHES

O nce as I stepped into the bar at the railway station in Majori, a little seaside town near Riga, my gaze fell on a lean old unshaven man in a clumsily patched jacket.

Winter gales swept in howling sheets over the Gulf of Riga. Thick ice rimmed the margin of the water and through the snowy mists came the sound of the surf.

The old man had evidently come into the bar to warm himself. He had not ordered anything and was sitting with a lost look on a wooden bench in the corner of the bar, his hands stuck into the sleeves of his jacket. A fluffy little white dog shivering with cold pressed close to his leg.

At a nearby table sat a group of young men drinking beer. The snow on their hats was melting and the drops of water tricked into their glasses and on to their smoked-sausage sandwiches. But the young men, heatedly discussing a football match, noticed nothing.

When one of them put half of his sandwich into his mouth, the dog could stand it no longer. It toddled over to the table, rose on its hind legs and looked imploringly into the mouth of the young man.

"Peti!" the old man called softly. "Aren't you ashamed of yourself? Why do you bother the young man?"

Peti did not budge. Its forelegs trembled and drooped on to its wet belly but it shook off its weariness and raised them again. The young men were engrossed in their talk and, pouring more and more cold beer into their glasses, did not notice the dog.

I wondered how they could drink ice-cold beer in such frosty weather with the windows all coated in snow.

"Peti!" the old man called again. "Peti, come right here!"

In answer the little dog wagged its tail several times, evidently to make the old man understand that it had heard him but couldn't help itself. And Peti avoided its master's eyes. It seemed to want to say: "I know what I'm doing is bad. But you are poor and you can't afford to buy me a sandwich like that, can you?"

"Oh, Peti, Peti!" the old man whispered and his voice quivered with disappointment.

Peti again wagged its tail and cast a quick imploring glance at the old man. It was as though it begged the old man not to call it or put it to shame any more, for it felt out of sorts as it was, and only extreme need had made it stoop to this business of begging from strangers.

At last one of the young men—he had high cheek-bones and wore a green hat—noticed the dog.

"Begging, you wretch? And where's your master?" he said.

The dog now wagged its tail joyfully, cast a sidelong glance at its master and yelped.

"Well, you're a fine one, citizen!" said the young man. "Keeping a dog and not feeding it properly, that won't do! Look, it's begging and begging's against the law."

The young men burst into laughter.

"That was a mouthful, Valentin!" yelled one of them and threw a piece of sausage to the dog.

"Don't dare touch it!" shouted the old man from his place, his weather-beaten face and thin bulbous neck reddening.

The animal slunk away without even so much as a glance at the sausage and, lowering its tail, went back to the old man.

"Not a crumb from them, hear that!" its master said.

And at once he began fumbling nervously in his pockets and, drawing from them a few grimy coins, counted these, carefully brushing the dirt off with trembling hands. The young man with the high cheek-bones passed another rude remark at the old man's expense, for which he was told off by his companions. Beer was again poured into the glasses.

Walking up to the counter, the old man put his handful of small change on it.

"One sandwich, please," he said hoarsely.

The little dog was at his side, its tail between its legs.

Two sandwiches lay on the plate which the counter girl passed to him.

"I only asked for one," said the old man.

"Never mind, take the two, it won't matter much to me," said the girl gently.

"*Paldies*," he said. "Thank you."

Taking the sandwiches, he stepped out of the bar, and found himself on the deserted railway platform. A squall had just swept past and another was coming but it was still far away on the horizon. Faint rays of sunlight coloured the white woods across the Lielupe River. Sitting down on a bench, the old man gave Peti one sandwich, the other he wrapped in a crumpled handkerchief and thrust into his pocket.

"Peti, Peti, what a stupid creature you are," said the old man as he watched the little dog quiver over the sandwich.

It paid no heed to his words but continued to eat while the old man wiped his eyes with his sleeve. They were tearing from the wind.

I have described the little scene I witnessed in Majori not because there is anything remarkable about it but because it focuses attention on details and little touches. Without these the whole atmosphere of the scene would be lost. There is the dog's apologetic air which supplies the pathetic touch. Leave out this and other little details such as the clumsily patched coat suggesting a lonely, perhaps widowed, life, the drops of thawed snow, trickling down from the young men's hats, the ice-cold beer, the coins, grimy from the scraps in the old man's pocket, and even the wind rolling in white sheets from the sea, and the story will sound rather crude.

In the fiction of recent years, particularly in the works of our young writers, we find less and less of the little touches that give atmosphere. Without them, a story loses all its flavour. It becomes as dry as the smoking rod from which the fat salmon had been removed, as Chekhov had once said. Details are needed, according to Pushkin, to draw attention and bring into sharp focus important trifles which otherwise escape notice.

On the other hand, there are writers who go to extremes and overburden their work with tedious superfluous details. They do not understand that a detail has a right to existence only when it is typical, when it helps to shed light on a character or a circumstance.

For example, to give the reader a picture of starting rain one might say that the first drops pattered loudly on a crumpled newspaper lying beneath the window.

144

Or, one may convey the tragedy of death in the manner that Alexei Tolstoi does in his novel *Ordeal*.

Dasha, one of the principal characters of the book, falls asleep exhausted. When she wakes up her baby is dead and the fluffy little hairs on its head are standing on end.

" 'While I slept death came to him...' Dasha said with tears to Telegin. 'Think of it, his hair's stood on end. He's suffered by himself, while I slept.'

"And no amount of persuasion could dispel the vision she had of her baby wrestling alone with death."

The one little touch (the baby's fluffy hair standing on end) proved more effective than a whole lot of detailed description.

A detail should be mentioned only if it is essential to the whole. Details must be picked and sifted very carefully before they fall in with the pattern of what we are writing. This is a process in which we rely upon our intuition. And intuition is that which assists the writer to reconstruct a whole picture from a single particular. Intuition helps the historical novelist to recreate the atmosphere of a past age, the mental attitudes and ways of thinking of the people of that age. It helped Pushkin who had been neither to England nor to Spain to write splendid poetry about Spain in his *The Stone Guest* and to paint a picture of England in his *Feast During the Plague* no less vivid than that by many well-known English writers.

An effective detail will help the reader to build up in his mind a complete picture of what the writer wants him to see—a character, an emotional state, an event or perhaps even a whole historical period.

"WHITE NIGHTS"

 tarting from the pier at Voznesenye our boat lurched into the waters of Lake Onega. Here amidst the woods and lakes of the North—and not above the Neva or Leningrad's palaces—I saw the "white nights." Hanging low in the eastern sky was the pale moon, its light diffused in the pearly whiteness of the night.

The waves churned by the steamer rolled noiselessly away, bits of pine bark rocking on their crests. On the shore the caretaker of an old church was striking the hour—twelve strokes. The sounds reached us from a great distance and were borne farther across the water's surface into the silvery night.

There is a magic beauty and a peculiar charm about these "white nights" of ivory twilight and fairy glimmer of gold and silver which it is hard to define. But they fill me with sadness because like all beautiful things they are so short-lived.

I was making my first trip to the North, yet everything seemed familiar to me, especially the heaps of white bird-cherry blossoms, withering that late spring in the neglected gardens. These fragrant cool blossoms were in abundance in Voznesenye. Yet nobody seemed to care to pick them and put them in bowls to adorn tables—perhaps because their season was over and they were fading.

I was on my way to Petrozavodsk. It was the year when Gorky thought of publishing a series of books under the general title of *History of Factories and Works*. He drew many writers into the work. It was decided that the writers would form teams—quite a new thing in literature.

From a number of factories suggested by Gorky I picked the Petrovsky Works in Petrozavodsk. These, I knew, had been started by Peter I as a forge for making cannon and anchors. Later they were turned into a copperworks and after the Revolution began producing road machinery.

I refused to join a writer's team for I was firmly convinced then, as I am convinced now, that while team work may be fruitful in many fields, it should not be practised in literature. At best, a team of writers can produce a collection of stories, but not one intergrated book. To my mind a literary work must bear the imprint of the writer's personality, express his reactions to reality, must be individual in style and language. Just as it is impossible for three persons to play the same violin, so, I held, it was impossible to write a book collectively.

When I told all this to Gorky, he winced, drummed on the table with his fingers, as was his habit, thought a little and replied:

"See, young man, that you don't get a reputation for being too self-confident. But off you go, write your book. Don't let us down, that's all!"

On the boat I recalled these words and felt that I must not let anything stand in the way of my writing the promised book. The North had a strong attraction for me and that, I hoped, would make my work easier. I could bring into my book that which charmed me most in the northern scene—white nights, still waters, forests, bird-cherry blossoms, the singsong Novgorod dialect, black ships with bent prows resembling swans' necks and painted yokes for carrying buckets of water.

Petrozavodsk, with huge moss-covered boulders lying here and there in the streets, was not densely populated at the time I arrived. The white gleam of the nearby lake and the pearly sky overhead gave the town a glazed aspect.

At once I went to the library and archives, reading everything that had any bearing on the Petrovsky Works. The history of the works proved devious and interesting. It involved Peter I, Scottish engineers, talented Russian serf gunsmiths, special ways of smelting metal, old-time customs—all of it fine material for my book.

After having done a good deal of reading I went to spend a few days in the village of Kizhi near the Kivach waterfall where stands the most beautifully designed wooden church in the world.

The Kivach roared and pine logs were borne down by its gleaming waters. I saw the church at sunset, thinking that it needed centuries to erect anything so fine and delicate and that none could do it but the hands of jewellers. Yet I knew that it was built by simple carpenters and within the usual space of time required for such a structure.

During my trip through this northern country I saw countless lakes and woods, cool sunshine and bleak vistas, but few people.

In Petrozavodsk I had made an outline for my future book. Into it went much history and many descriptions— but few people.

I decided to write the book in Petrozavodsk and rented a room in the home of a one-time schoolmistress. She

was an unobtrusive elderly woman called Serafima Ivanovna with not a vestige of the schoolmistress left in her
now, except for the spectacles she wore and a smat-
tering of French.

I settled down to write with my outline before me but
soon found I could work no cohesion into my material. It
crumbled right there before my eyes. Interesting bits
dangled like loose ends unwilling to be tied up to adjoining bits no less interesting. The facts I had dug up
from the archives would not hang together. There seemed
to be nothing that could breathe life into them, no real
local colour and no living personality.

I kept writing about machines, production, foremen
and other things—but with a deep melancholy, for the
story lacked something very important, something into
which I could put my heart: a human touch, without
which I knew there would be no book at all.

By the way, it was at that time that I realized that you
must write about machines the same way as you write
about people—feel their pulse beat, love them, penetrate
into their life. I always feel physical pain when a machine
is abused. For example when a Pobeda strains on a steep
incline I feel no less exhausted than the car. Writers
when describing machines must treat them with the same
consideration as human beings. I have noticed that this
is a good workman's attitude to his tools.

An inability to shape one's material is frightfully dis-
concerting to a writer.

I felt like one who was doing something entirely out
of his line—as though I were dancing in a ballet or
editing the philosophy of Kant. Gorky's admonition
"Don't let us down" came painfully back to me. I was
depressed yet for another reason: one of my own maxims
in regard to writing was crumbling, for I held that a

writer worthy of the name should be able to make a story out of any kind of material.

In this state of mind I decided to give up writing the book and leave Petrozavodsk.

There was nobody I could carry my disappointment to but Serafima Ivanovna. I was just on the point of confiding in her, when it appeared that with the intuition of a schoolmistress she had herself noticed what my trouble was.

"You remind me of some of my foolish girl pupils who went to pieces before the examination," she said to me. "They would stuff their heads so that they soon failed to distinguish the important from the trifling. Yours is a case of fatigue. I don't know much about your profession, still I think that writers should never force themselves to write. Don't leave the town. Rest a while till you feel more fit. Go down to the lake. Take a walk round the town, you'll find it a pleasant place. Perhaps that'll set you right."

My decision to leave Petrozavodsk was not shaken, but I saw no harm in roaming round the town with which I had not yet had an opportunity to become more closely acquainted.

After walking for some time northward along the lake I found myself on the outskirts, where there were extensive vegetable gardens. Among these, here and there, I caught glimpses of crosses and tombstones. Puzzled, I asked an old man who was weeding a carrot patch whether they were the remains of an old graveyard.

"Yes," he replied, "a graveyard for foreigners. Now the land's used for growing vegetables and the tombstones are crumbling away. The few that are left are not likely to survive till next spring."

I could see that no more than five or six stones had remained. One, fenced off by a wrought-iron railing of beautiful workmanship, attracted my attention. On approaching it I found an age-worn granite tombstone with an inscription in French, almost hidden from view by the tall burdock that grew around it. I broke the burdock and read: "Here lies Charles Eugène Longceville, artillery engineer of Emperor Napoleon's Grand Army, born in 1778, in Perpignan, died in the summer of 1816 in Petrozavodsk, far from his native land. May he rest in peace."

I realized that here was a man with a romantic history and that he would be my saving.

On returning to my room I told Serafima Ivanovna that I had changed my mind about leaving Petrozavodsk and went at once to the town archives. There I was met by the custodian, formerly a teacher of mathematics. He was a shrivelled-up bespectacled old man so thin that he seemed almost transparent. The filing in the archives had not been completed but the custodian knew his way about very well. When I told him what I wanted he grew quite excited. Here was something that was not dull routine, mostly consisting of digging up old records in church registers, but really interesting work—a search for papers that may throw light on the fate of an officer of Napoleon's army who had in some mysterious fashion landed in the north of Russia in Petrozavodsk more than a century ago and there met his death.

It was not without misgivings as to its outcome that we began our search. What could we hope to find about Longceville that would make it possible to reconstruct with some feasibility the story of his life? Could we, in fact, hope to find anything?

In his eagerness to help, the custodian declared that he would spend the night at the archives and go through as many papers as he could very thoroughly in the hope of finding what I needed. I would have stayed with him too, had it not been against the rules. Instead I went down town, bought a loaf of bread, some sausage, tea and sugar and, after leaving it with the custodian so that he could have a snack in the night, went home.

The search went on for ten days. Every morning the custodian would show me a pile of documents which he thought might contain some mention of Longceville. In mathematical fashion he marked off the most important of these with the radical sign. On the seventh day of the search we came across a record of the burial of Charles Eugène Longceville in the Cemetery Register. From it we learned that he had been a prisoner of war in Russia and that somewhat unusual circumstances attended his burial. The ninth day yielded two private letters in which reference was made to Longceville and the tenth a report, partly torn and with no signature, of the Olonets Governor-General on the brief sojourn in Petrozavodsk "of Marie Cécile Trinité, the wife of the above-mentioned Longceville, who arrived from France to erect a tombstone over the grave of her deceased husband."

That was all that the obliging custodian was able to provide me with, but it was enough to make Longceville come alive in my imagination.

And as soon as I had a picture of Longceville in my mind, all the material on the history of the works which but a short while ago was a disorderly mass suddenly shaped itself into a smooth tale. I named my story "The Fate of Charles Longceville" for it was all built around Longceville. This Charles Longceville was a veteran of the French Revolution, who was taken prisoner by the Cossacks at Gzhatsk and exiled to the territory of the Petrozavodsk Works where he died of an attack of fever.

The material was dead until a personality appeared.

And when that happened my old outline went to pieces. Longceville became the central figure of the story. I drew him against the background of the historical facts

I had collected. And much of what I had seen in the North was incorporated into the story.

There is a scene of lamentation over Longceville's dead body described in my book which was taken from life and has quite a history of its own.

I happened to be taking a boat trip up the Svir from Lake Ladoga to Lake Onega when a pine coffin was lifted from the pier on to the boat's lower deck. It appeared that one of the oldest and most experienced pilots on the Svir had died. And as a last tribute his friends were taking him on a farewell voyage down the whole length of the river he loved, from Sviritsa to Voznesenye. This gave the inhabitants along the shore, who esteemed the pilot and among whom he enjoyed great popularity, the opportunity to pay their last respects to him.

The dead man belonged to that gallant brotherhood of pilots who employed all their wits and skill to steer boats safely down the dangerous rapids of the swift-flowing Svir. Among these brave men existed bonds of the strongest friendship.

As we were now passing the region of the rapids, and going upstream two tug-boats came to the assistance of our boat, though its engines were turning at full speed. Boats going downstream also had tug-boats—but behind them to slow them down and to avoid getting caught in the rapids.

Inhabitants all along the shore were informed by telegraph that the remains of the deceased pilot were on board the boat. And at every landing-stage crowds of people came to meet the boat. In front stood old women in black shawls. As soon as the boat reached the bank they broke into a high-pitched wail uttering lamentations. At every port of call down to Voznesenye this scene repeated itself. But each time the lamentations were differently worded, improvised on the spur of the moment.

At Voznesenye a group of pilots came aboard and lifted the lid of the coffin, revealing the weather-beaten face of a powerfully built grey-haired old mariner.

Raised on linen towels, the coffin was carried ashore amidst loud wailing. A young woman walked behind the coffin, covering her pale face with a shawl and holding a little fair-haired boy by the hand. A few steps behind followed a man of about forty in a river-boat captain's uniform. They were the daughter, grandson and son-in-law of the deceased.

The boat lowered its flag and when the coffin was conveyed to the graveyard its whistle blew several blasts.

In my story there is a description of the planet Venus at its brightest, exactly as I had seen it myself. It is something that has come to be associated in my mind with the northern scene. In no other part of the world have I even noticed Venus. But here I watched her gain full and peerless brilliancy, as lustrous as a gem in the greenish sky with the dawn just breaking, shining in all her splendour, an unrivalled queen of the firmament, over the northern lakes of Ladoga and Onega.

FOUNTAIN-HEAD OF ART

n the company of a few friends Emile Zola had once said that a writer can well dispense with imagination and should rely on his powers of observation alone, as he did himself.

"Yet you yourself have been known to read but a single newspaper item and it had set you off on such a long and devious train of thought that without leaving your home for months you have produced a voluminous novel. Had imagination nothing to do with it?" asked Maupassant who happened to be among the company.

Zola did not reply. Maupassant took his hat and left, caring little that his sudden departure might seem discourteous. He would have no one, not even Zola, reject imagination, which he valued highly, as do most writers, as do you and I.

Imagination is the rich soil from which spring poetry and prose, and all creative thought, the great fountainhead of art, "its eternal sun and god," as the poets of the Latin Quarter used to say.

But the dazzling sun of imagination glows only when in close proximity to the earth. Away from the earth it loses its luminosity. Its light fails.

What is imagination? A difficult question to answer. "Quite a poser," as my friend Arkady Gaidar would have said.

To get to the bottom of things which are not easily explained one should perhaps be as stubborn as children when they want an answer to their questions.

"What is it? What's it for?" they ask and then follow up their questions with a string of others. And there is no putting them off. You must make an effort to give at least some plausible answers.

Now supposing a child asks: "And what is imagination?" hardly able to pronounce that long word.

To define imagination by some vague phrase as "the sun of art" or "the holy of holies" would only lead us into sophistries and in the end we would be forced to flee from our young interlocutor.

Children demand clarity. Perhaps the easiest way to begin to answer this question is to say that imagination is a property of the human mind which enables man, by bringing into play his store of observations, his thoughts and feelings, to create alongside the real world an imaginary one with imaginary persons and events. (All this must be worded much simpler.)

"But what do you need an imaginary world for, isn't the real world good enough?" we may be asked.

"Because the real world and real life are far too vast and complicated for man ever to comprehend them in their entirety and multiplicity. And besides, a good deal that is or was real is beyond man's power to see and experience. For example, a man living in the present age cannot transport himself three centuries back and become a student of Galileo, participate in the capture of Paris in 1814; or, sitting in Moscow, touch the marble columns of Acropolis; or converse with Gogol; or sit in the Convention and listen to Marat's speeches; or watch the Pacific Ocean and the star-studded sky above it from aboard a ship—when one has never even set eyes on the sea. And a man longs to learn, see, hear and experience everything. That is where the gift of imagination comes in, filling in the gaps in one's experiences."

At this stage of our discussion we may begin to discuss things that are beyond our young interlocutor's comprehension.

For example, can a sharp line be drawn between imagining and thinking? No!

Newton's law of gravity, the sad story of Tristan and Isolt, the theory of atomic fission, the beautiful building of the former Admiralty in Leningrad, Levitan's landscape *Golden Autumn, The Marseillaise*, radio, electric light, the personality of Hamlet, the theory of relativity and the film *Bambi* are all products of the imagination.

Human thought without imagination can yield nothing, just as imagination is sterile when it is divorced from reality.

"Great thoughts are rooted in the heart," goes a French saying. It would be more exact to say that great thoughts are rooted in our whole being. Our entire being contributes to the birth of these thoughts. The heart, imagination and reason—in these lies the seat of what we call culture. And something that even our most powerful imagination cannot imagine is the extinction of imagination and everything which it has created. When imagination is dead, man will cease to be man.

Imagination is nature's great gift to man. It is inherent in human nature.

Imagination, as I have already said, is dead without reality but it, in its turn, may affect reality, that is the course of our life, our deeds and thoughts and our attitudes to the people who surround us. If human beings could not visualize the future, wrote the critic Pisarev, they would never build patiently for that future, fight stubbornly and even sacrifice their lives for it.

> Perchance on your penknife you'll find
> A speck of dust from lands afar,
> The world will once again arise
> Mysterious, wrapped in veil bizarre...

wrote Alexander Blok. Another poet had said:

> In every puddle—fragrance of the ocean,
> In every stone—a breath of desert sands...

A grain of sand from a distant land, a stone on a highway—often such things set our imagination working. This calls to mind the story of a certain Spanish hidalgo.

The hidalgo was a poor nobleman living in Castille on his ancestral estate, which consisted of but a small piece of land and a gloomy-looking stone house resembling a prison. He was a lonely man, the one other creature in the house being the old nurse of the family, now quite in her dotage. She was able with difficulty to prepare his meagre meals but it was useless to make conversation with her. And so the hidalgo would spend most of his day sitting in a time-worn armchair by his lancet window and reading, only the crackling of the dry glue on the books' backs breaking the silence. Now and then his gaze would rest on the scene beyond the window. What he saw was a withered black tree and a monotonous view of plains stretching to the horizon. The landscape in the part of Spain where he lived was desolate and cheerless but the hidalgo was accustomed to it.

He was no longer of an age when he could abandon

his hearth for the discomforts of long, fatiguing journeys. Besides, in the whole of the kingdom he had neither relations nor friends. Little was known of his past. It was said he had had a wife and a beautiful daughter, but that both had been carried away by the plague in the same month of the same year. Since then he had led a secluded life, even loth to extend his hospitality to stray wanderers by night or in inclement weather.

Yet one day when a stranger with a weather-beaten face, a homespun cloak flung over his shoulders, knocked on the door of the hidalgo's house, he welcomed him cordially. During supper, while they sat before the fire, he told the hidalgo that—blessed be the Madonna—he had returned safe and sound from a perilous voyage to the west where the king, persuaded by a certain Italian called Columbus, had sent several carvels.

They sailed the ocean for weeks. In the open sea the mariners were tempted by the sweet songs of the Sirens who asked to be taken aboard to warm themselves and to wrap their nude bodies in their long hair as in blankets. When the captain ordered his men to pay no heed to the Sirens, the mariners, sick with longing for love, for the touch of firm rounded female hips, rose against him. The mutiny ended in the defeat of the mariners, three of the ringleaders being hanged from the ship's yard-arm.

They sailed on until they sighted a marvellous sea all overgrown with weeds in which bloomed large dark-blue flowers. Mass was held, and when the ship began to sail round this sea of grass a new land, unknown and beautiful, burst into view. From its shores the wind carried the murmur of the woods and the intoxicating scent of flowers. Mounting the quarter-deck, the captain raised his sword skywards, the tip of the blade flashing brightly in the sun. This was a sign that they had discovered the wonderful land of Eldorado, rich in precious gems and gleaming with mountains of gold and silver.

The hidalgo listened in silence to the stranger. The latter on taking leave drew from his leather bag a pink seashell brought from the land of Eldorado and presented it to the elderly hidalgo in token of gratitude for his supper and bed. It was a worthless thing and so the hidalgo had no scruples in accepting it.

On the night after the stranger departed a storm broke, lightning streaking the sky above the rocky plains.

The sea-shell lay on the hidalgo's bedside table. And as he awoke in the night he beheld deep in the shell a vision of a fairy land of roseate hue, of foam and of clouds, caught in the glow of the lightning. The lightning was gone, but the hidalgo waited for the next flash and again he beheld the wonderful land, now more distinctly than the first time. He saw broad cascades of water, frothing and gleaming as they rolled down steep banks into the sea. These, he supposed, were rivers. And he thought he could feel their freshness and even the spray of water lightly brushing against his face.

Thinking that he must be dreaming, he rose, moved his armchair to the table, sat down in front of the seashell, bent over it, and with a beating heart, endeavoured to get a better view of the country he had seen. But the flashes of lightning grew less and less frequent and soon were no more.

He did not light a candle fearing that its rude light would reveal to him that he was suffering from an optical illusion. He sat up till the morning. In the rays of the rising sun the sea-shell did not appear at all remarkable. There was nothing in it except a smoky greyness into which the country he had seen seemed to have dissolved.

That same day the hidalgo went to Madrid and, kneeling before the king, implored him to give his consent for a carvel to be equipped at his own expense, so that he may sail to the west where he hoped to discover a new and wonderful land.

The king graciously gave his consent. But as soon as the hidalgo left his presence, he said to his attendants: "The hidalgo must be stark mad to hope to achieve anything with a single miserable carvel. Yet it is the Lord who guides the madman. For all we know he may yet annex some new land to our crown."

For months and months the hidalgo sailed westward, drinking nothing but water and eating very little. Agitation was wasting away his flesh. He tried hard not to think of his dream-land fearing that he may never reach it; or that after all it may turn out to be a monotonous table-land with nothing but prickly grass and wind-swept clouds of grey dust.

The hidalgo prayed to the Madonna that she may spare him the pain of such a disappointment. A crudely carved wooden image of the Madonna, her protuberant blue eyes gazing fixedly into the distant vistas of the sea, was attached to the prow of the carvel. Splashes glistened on the discoloured gold of the Madonna's hair and in the faded purple of her cloak.

"Lead us!" adjured the hidalgo. "It cannot be that such a land does not exist, for I see it as clearly in my waking hours as in my dreams."

And lo! one evening the mariners drew a broken twig from the water—a sign that land was near. The twig was covered with enormous leaves resembling an ostrich's feathers and having a sweet and refreshing scent. Not a single man on the carvel slept that night.

At dawn a land stretching from one end of the ocean to the other and gleaming with the tints of its wall of mountains came into view. Crystalline rivers flowed down the mountain slopes into the ocean. Flocks of bright-plumed birds, unable to penetrate into the woods because of the thick mass of foliage, whirled round the tree-tops. From the shore came the scent of flowers and fruits. And every breath of that scent seemed to bring immortality.

When the sun rose overhead, the land, bathed in the misty spray of its waterfalls, appeared in all the glory of the hues that the glint of playing sunbeams lends to a cut-glass vessel. It sparkled like a diamond girdle forgotten on the margin of the sea by the virgin goddess of heaven and light.

Falling on his knees and stretching his arms towards the unknown land, the hidalgo exclaimed: "I thank thee, oh Providence, for having filled my heart in the declining years of my life with a longing for adventure and made my soul pine for a blessed land which, hath it not been for thee, I might never have beheld, and my eyes would have dried up and grown blind from the monotonous view of the table-land. I wish to name this happy land after my daughter Florencia."

Scores of little rainbows sped towards the carvel from the shore and they made the hidalgo's head swim. The tiny rainbows gleamed in the sun and played in the many waterfalls. In reality they were not hurrying towards the carvel—the carvel was approaching them, its sails and the gay bunting hoisted by the crew fluttering jubilantly.

But suddenly the hidalgo fell face downwards upon the warm wet deck and did not stir. Life had gone out of him—the great joy of the day was too much for his weary heart and it burst.

Such, they say, is the story of the discovery of that stretch of land which later came to be known as Florida.

That imagination may at times exercise a certain power over reality itself is the point I have tried to make in the story about the hidalgo. It was the stranger in the homespun cloak who fired the hidalgo's imagination and launched him on a voyage of adventure which ended in a great discovery.

The remarkable thing about imagination is that it makes you believe in the reality of what you imagine. Without that belief, imagination would be nothing but a trick of the mind, a senseless, puerile kaleidoscope. And it is believing in the reality of what you imagine that has the power to make you seek it in life, to fight for its fulfilment, to do imagination's bidding as the elderly hidalgo had done, and finally—to clothe what you imagine with reality.

Imagination is primarily and most closely associated with the arts, with literature and poetry.

Imagination has its roots in memories and memories in reality. Memories are not stored up chaotically in the mind. They are held together by the law of association, or, as Mikhail Lomonosov called it, "the law of co-imagination," by which our memories are pigeon-holed in the recesses of the mind according to their similarity or proximity in time and space. In this way an uninterrupted, consistent train of associations is formed. It is this train of associations that guides imagination through its various channels.

For the writer his store of associations is extremely important. The larger it is, the richer his spiritual world.

Drop a twig, a nail or any other object into a bubbling mineral spring and see what happens. The object will in a short while become covered with myriads of tiny crystals, so beautifully shaped and intricately entwined as to be virtual works of art. Approximately, the same thing happens to our thoughts thrown into the midst of our memories, memories saturated with associations. They expand, grow rich and mature into real works of art.

Almost any object can evoke a train of associations.

But with each person that train of associations will be different, as different as his own life, experiences, and recollections are from those of other people. One and the same word calls forth different associations in different people. The task of the writer is to produce in the reader the same train of associations that obtains in his own mind.

Lomonosov in his *Rhetorics* cites a very simple example of how a train of associations is evoked. According to him, association is the human capacity to imagine along with one object others that are somehow connected with it. For example, when in our mind's eye we see a ship, we at once associate it with the sea on which it sails, the sea with a storm, the storm with waves, the waves with the surf breaking on the shore and the shore with pebbles.

This, of course, is a very simplified instance of association. Generally, associations are far more complicated.

Here is an example of a more complicated train of associations:

I was writing in a small house overlooking the Gulf of Riga. In the adjoining room, the Latvian poet Immermanis was reciting his poetry aloud. He was wearing a red knitted pullover. I remembered having seen Sergei Eisenstein, the film producer, wearing the same kind of pullover during the recent war. I had met him in the street in Alma-Ata. He was carrying a pile of books he had just bought. The books were oddly chosen. There were among them a manual on volley-ball, a book on the history of the Middle Ages, an algebra text-book and the novel *Tsushima* by Novikov-Priboi.

"It's a film producer's business to know a good deal if he wants to make good pictures," said Eisenstein.

"Even algebra?" I asked.

"Certainly," replied Eisenstein.

In thinking about Eisenstein I remembered that at the time I met him in Alma-Ata the poet Vladimir Lugovskoi was writing a long poem, a chapter of which went under the title of "Alma-Ata, City of Dreams," and was dedicated to Eisenstein. Some Mexican masks which hung in Eisenstein's rooms were described in the poem. He had brought these on his return from a trip to Central America. In Mexico, by the way, there is a tribe called Maya, which is now almost extinct. A few pyramid-shaped temples and half a dozen words of their language is practically all that remains. Legend has it that it was from parrots in the trackless forests of Yucatan that scholars first heard many of the words belonging to the language of the ancient tribe of Maya. These words were passed on from one generation of parrots to another.

The fate of this tribe led me to the conclusion that the history of the conquest of America was a blood-curdling record of human infamy. "Infamy," I thought next, was a good title for a historical novel. It's like a slap in the face.

What a tormenting business finding an appropriate title for a book is. One must have a talent for it. Some writers can write fine books but are helpless in choosing titles for them. With others it is just the opposite. The next minute I was already thinking of something else—of the host of literary men who were far better talkers than writers, draining themselves dry in conversation. Gorky was both a brilliant story-teller and a great writer. He had the gift of telling a story beautifully and afterwards writing down a new version of it. He needed but some slight event to start him off. He would enhance it with a wealth of detail and make of it a fascinating story which he liked repeating, each time adding fresh details, changing parts of it and making it each time more interesting. The stories he told were finished artistic creations in themselves. He enjoyed telling them but only to sympathetic listeners who understood and believed him. On the other hand, he was always annoyed by matter-of-fact, unimaginative people who doubted the truth of what he narrated. He would frown, grow silent and even say: "It's a dull world with people like you in it, comrades!"

Many writers have possessed the gift of building up a marvellous story around some fact or incident from real life. Here my thoughts turned from Gorky to Mark Twain, for he, too, possessed this gift to a remarkable degree. In this connection I remembered a story told about Mark Twain and a critic who accused the writer of mixing facts with fiction, or rather of plain lying. Mark Twain replied to the critic that it wouldn't be a bad idea for him to become closer acquainted with the "art of lying" if he wanted to be a judge of it.

The writer Ilya Ilf told me that in the little town where Mark Twain was born he saw a monument to Tom Sawyer and Huckleberry Finn, with Huck swinging a dead cat by the tail. Why shouldn't monuments be put up to the heroes of books, for example, to Don Quixote or Gulliver, or Pavel Korchagin from Ostrovsky's *How the Steel Was Tempered,* to Tatyana Larina, heroine of Pushkin's *Eugene Onegin,* to Gogol's Taras Bulba, to Pierre Bezukhov from Tolstoi's *War and Peace,* to Chekhov's three sisters, to Lermontov's Maxim Maximovich or Bella.

That is an example of how thoughts run in an endless chain of associations, from a red sweater to a monument to Bella, Lermontov's heroine.

I have devoted so much space to associations because they are so closely intertwined with creative patterns of thought. They feed the imagination, and without imagination literature cannot exist.

What Bestuzhev-Marlinsky said about imagination seems most apt to me.

"The chaos in our mind is the forerunner of the creation of something true, lofty and poetical. Let but the ray of genius penetrate that chaos and the hostile little particles will be vitalized in a process of love and harmony, drawn to the one which is strongest. They will join smoothly, form a gleaming pattern of crystals, and will flow in a stream of vigorous writing."

Night gradually sets into motion the powers of the soul. What are these powers? The working of the imagination which lets a flood of fantasy loose from the tiny recesses of my consciousness? The soul's rapture or its peace? Do they spring from joy or sorrow? Who knows?

I extinguished the lamp and the darkness began to fade, tinged by the white glint of snow from the ice-bound gulf which, like a huge, tarnished looking-glass, cast its phantom glimmer upon the night.

I could see the black crowns of the Baltic pines etched against the sky and hear the distant rumble of passing electric trains. But soon all grew quiet again, so quiet that the ear could catch the slightest rustle among the pine branches, and even some strange faint crackling, coinciding with the flashes of the stars. It was as though rime was breaking off the stars, gently cracking and tinkling.

I· lived alone in a deserted house by the sea which stretched for hundreds of miles. Beyond the dunes were endless bogs and stunted copses. There was not a soul anywhere. But as soon as I relighted the lamp, sat down at my desk and resumed my writing, no matter what about, the feeling of solitude left me. I was no longer alone. I felt in my room the presence of thousands of readers to whom I could speak, whom I could rouse at my will to laughter, meditation, love, anger, compassion, whom I could take by the hand and lead along the pathways of life, created here within the four walls of my room, but breaking through them to become universal.

To lead them forward to the dawn—the dawn which was certain to come and was already lifting the veil of night and touching the sky with the faintest tinge of blue.

I sat at my desk not knowing what I would write. I was in a state of agitation; my thoughts were vague. I had but the longing to convey to others that which filled my mind, my heart and my whole being. What form my thoughts would take, in what channels they would flow, I did not know myself.

Yet I knew for whom I would write. I would make the whole world my audience. But it was difficult and almost impossible to visualize anything so vast. Hence I thought, as I usually do, of some one individual—a little girl with beautifully sparkling eyes who had a few days ago run to meet me as I was crossing a meadow. When she was at my side, she caught me by the elbow.

"I've been waiting for you here for a long time," she said, pausing for breath. "I've picked flowers and have recited Chapter II from *Eugene Onegin* nine times. I want to fetch you home. Everybody's expecting you there. We feel dull without you, and we're dying to hear about one of your adventures by the lake. Please think up something exciting. But then you needn't think it up at all but tell about things that really happened. It's so glorious in the meadows with briar-rose blooming afresh. Oh, it's so good!"

And perhaps it was not for this little girl at all that I was writing but for the woman whose life through long years of hardship, joy and tenderness has been so closely bound up with mine that we have learned to fear nothing. And perhaps it was for my friends, mostly of my own age, whose ranks were beginning to thin. But I was really writing for all who cared to read me.

I did not know what to write, because I had ever so much to say and had not as yet sifted my thoughts to get at that which is most important and which helps all the rest to fall in with it.

The state I have described is familiar to all who write.

"There comes a moment bringing with it a longing to write—you do not know what about but you feel that you will write," Turgenev said. "This is a mood which poets call the approach of God, the artist's one moment of rapture. Were there no such moment, no one would care to write. Later, when you have to fit your thoughts into a pattern and put them down on paper, the period of torment begins."

While I was still thinking of what to write, the quiet was suddenly broken by the far-off siren of a steamer. What was a steamer doing here, in the ice-bound waters? Then I remembered having read in yesterday's newspaper that an ice-breaker had left Leningrad for the Gulf of Riga. That explained the siren.

Then a story once told to me by an ice-breaker pilot of how in the Gulf of Finland he had caught sight of a bunch of field flowers frozen to the ice, came to my mind. I wondered who had lost them in the desolate snow-fields. They may have been dropped from a passing steamer when it was making its way through thin ice.

The bunch of frozen flowers—that image ready in my mind, I began to write. I knew there must be some explanation for the flowers being where they were. Everyone who saw them would no doubt put forward his own conjecture. I had not seen the flowers but I, too, had an idea of why they were there. Why could they not be the same bunch of flowers picked in the meadow by the little girl who ran to meet me? I felt certain that they were the self-same flowers. How did they come to be on the ice? To answer that was easy enough, for anything can happen in a story.

Here the thought came to my mind that the female attitude to flowers is different from the male. To men, flowers are merely decorative things. Women regard them more tenderly, associating them with romance rather than adornment.

With regret I watched the approach of dawn. Daylight often divests our thoughts of their romance. Many stories have a tendency to shrink in the sunlight, retiring like snails into their shells.

My story had not yet taken shape in my mind. But it was there. I knew it would develop of its own accord. To prevent its developing would be nothing short of infanticide.

It was as difficult to write it as to convey the faint scent of grass. Yet I wrote quickly with bated breath, so as not to blow away the thin cobweb in which the story was enveloped, not to miss the play of light and shade and the mental pictures that flash into the mind and soon vanish, not to lag behind the flow of imagination.

The story was finished at last, and I longed to look with gratitude into those beautiful sparkling eyes with their eager, never-fading light in which it gleamed immortal.

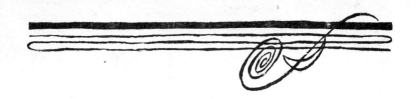

THE NIGHT COACH

I had planned to devote another chapter in this book to imagination, but on second thought decided to write a story about Hans Christian Andersen which, I think, may well take the place of such a chapter and serve to illustrate the power of imagination better than general statements on the subject.

t was no use asking for ink in the poky, tumbledown hotel in Venice. Why should they keep any in stock—to make out the inflated bills they presented to their residents?

True, when Hans Christian Andersen moved to the hotel, he did find a little ink at the bottom of the ink-well on his table. He began to write a fairy-tale. But the poor fairy-tale—it was fading right before his eyes because to keep the small supply of ink from running dry water had to be added all the time. Because there was no ink left to finish it, the tale's happy ending remained at the bottom of the ink-well. That amused Andersen and he even thought of calling his next story "The Tale Left at the Bottom of the Dry Ink-Well."

171

Meanwhile, Andersen had learned to love Venice and called it "the fading lotus flower." He watched the low autumn clouds curl over the sea and the fetid water splash in the canals while a cold wind whistled in the street corners. Whenever the sunlight broke through the clouds and the rose-coloured marble of the walls gleamed from under their coating of mould, the city, as Andersen saw it from his window, looked like a picture by Canaletto, one of the old Venetian masters, beautiful, yet somewhat melancholy.

The time came for him to leave and continue his travels through Italy. Without regret he sent the hotel servant to buy a ticket for the coach leaving that evening for Verona.

Lazy, always slightly tipsy, the servant, though he seemed frank and simple-minded, was a rogue at heart who fitted the hotel very well. He had not once even swept the stone floor in Andersen's room, let alone cleaned the room itself. And it was a sorry place indeed. Moths swarmed from the red velvet curtains. For washing there was a cracked porcelain bowl with painted figures of bathers. The oil-lamp was broken, a heavy silver candelabrum with a candle end in it serving in its stead. And the candelabrum looked as though it had not been cleaned since the time of Titian.

On the ground floor of the hotel was a dingy kitchen, smelling of roast mutton and garlic. All day long young women in torn, carelessly laced velvet corsages could be heard, now laughing loudly, now quarrelling noisily. Their squabbles would at times end up with the women clawing into each other's hair. At such moments, Andersen, if he happened to be passing by, stopped and looked with amused admiration at the young women's tousled hair, at their flaming faces, their eyes burning with a thirst for vengeance, and at the tears of anger flowing down their pretty cheeks.

Embarrassed by the presence of the lean, thin-nosed, elegantly dressed gentleman, the young women would stop quarrelling at once. They took Andersen for a travelling conjuror though they respectfully addressed him as "Signor poet." He did not answer to their conception of a poet. He was not hot-blooded. He did not play the guitar and sing the romantic songs of the gondolier. Nor did he fall in love with every pretty woman he met. Only once did he take the red rose from his button-hole and toss it to the ugliest girl among the dish-washers, who was furthermore lame.

No sooner had he sent the hotel servant off for the ticket than he went to the window and drew the curtain. He watched the fellow saunter down the edge of the canal and heard him whistle. Passing by a red-cheeked woman selling fish, he pinched her in her full bosom and got a sound slap in return. Then he saw the scamp spitting long and earnestly into the canal from the top of a humped bridge, taking aim at a split egg-shell floating in the water; at last he hit the mark and the shell disappeared under the water. He next strolled up to an urchin in a tattered cap who was fishing, and stared at the floating rod, waiting for a fish to bite.

"O Lord!" cried Andersen in despair. "This rascal will prevent my leaving Venice tonight!"

And he flung open the window with such force that the sound of rattling glass reached the servant's ears. As the fellow raised his head, Andersen brandished two angry fists. The servant seized the boy's cap, waved it joyously at Andersen, then, clapping it back on the boy's head, sprang to his feet and disappeared round the corner.

Andersen burst into laughter. He was no longer angry. The fellow was a rogue but he was amusing and quite a character. To him little incidents like that were the spice of travel, a pastime of which he was growing fonder and fonder.

Travelling had so much excitement in store for one—a significant glance from behind pretty lashes, the towers of an unfamiliar town suddenly looming into view, the masts of great ships swaying on the horizon, violent storms in the Alps, some charming voice, like the tingling of a wayside bell, singing of young love.

The servant brought a ticket for the coach but no change. Andersen seized him by the scruff of the neck and pushed him gently out of the room. There, laughing, he gave him a punch and the fellow went darting down the shaky stairway, skipping steps and singing at the top of his voice.

As the coach started from Venice, it began to drizzle and a pitch blackness stole over the country; the coachman remarked that it was the devil's own idea to travel by night from Venice to Verona.

When the passengers made no reply he kept silent for a while, spat, and then warned them that but for the little piece now burning in the lantern he had no candles. His words again evoking no comment, he next expressed a doubt of the sanity of his passengers, adding that Verona was a poky hole and no place for decent folk. No one objected to what he said, though all knew how untrue his words were.

There were only three passengers in the coach—Andersen, an elderly morose-looking priest, and a lady wrapped in a dark cloak who in the deceptive flickering of the candle-light one moment seemed young and beautiful to Andersen and the next old and ugly.

"Don't you think we had better put out the candle?" said Andersen. "We can do without it now and ought to save it for an emergency."

"That's an idea that would never enter the head of an Italian!" exclaimed the priest.

"Why?"

"Italians are incapable of thinking ahead. They let things slide until they are beyond repair."

"Evidently the Reverend gentleman does not belong to that light-hearted nation?" Andersen remarked.

"I'm an Austrian," the priest replied sullenly.

That closed the conversation and Andersen blew out the candle.

"In this part of Italy it is safer to ride by night without the candle burning," said the lady, after a long pause.

"The rumbling of the wheels will betray us just as well," objected the priest, and added stiffly, "ladies have no business travelling by night without a chaperon."

"The gentleman sitting next to me is as good as a chaperon," replied the lady and laughed archly.

Andersen removed his hat to acknowledge the honour.

No sooner was the candle out than the sounds and smells of the night grew more distinct, as though happy in the disappearance of a rival. The clatter of the horses' hoofs, the crunching of the wheels against the road, the creaking of the springs and the drumming of the rain on the coach-roof were all louder now, and the smell of moist grass coming from the open window seemed more tart.

"Strange!" muttered Andersen. "I expected Italy to smell of wild oranges, but I recognize the smell of my own northern land."

"The air will change as soon as we begin going uphill," said the lady. "It will get warmer."

The horses slowed their pace. There was a steep ascent ahead. Under the spreading branches of the age-old elms rimming both sides of the road, the night was blacker than ever. There was a profound peace broken only by the faint rustling of the leaves and the patter of rain.

Andersen lowered the window, letting the elm boughs swing into the coach. He tore a few leaves off a twig for a souvenir.

Like many people with a vivid imagination, he had a passion for collecting all sorts of trifles on his travels, such as bits of mosaic, an elm-leaf, a tiny donkey-shoe, all having the power to re-create later the mood he had been in when he picked them up.

"Night-time!" said Andersen to himself.

The gloom of the night helped him to give himself up wholly to his reveries. And when he wearied of them, he could think up stories with himself as their young, handsome hero, making lavish use of the intoxicating phrases which sentimental critics call the "flowers of poetry." It was nice to think of himself as such, when in reality—and he did not deceive himself—he was extremely unattractive, lanky, shy, his arms and legs dangling like those of a toy jumping-man. He could not hope to win the disposition of the fair sex. And he smarted with pain when young pretty girls passed him by with about as much attention as they would give to a lamp-post.

Andersen fell to drowsing but he soon awoke and the first thing that caught his eye was a green star gleaming low over the horizon. He knew it was the early hours of the morning.

The coach had halted and Andersen could hear the coachman haggling over the fare with some young women whose coaxing tones were so melodious that they reminded him of the music of an old opera he had once heard. They were asking for a lift to a nearby town but could not pay the fare demanded of them though they had pooled their resources and were ready to give them all to the coachman.

"Enough!" cried Andersen to the coachman. "I'll pay the remainder of the sum you are knave enough to demand from the young ladies, only stop your stupid haggling!"

"Very well, get in, pretty ladies, get in," grumbled the coachman, "and thank the gracious Madonna for having sent a foreign prince with plenty of money your way. And don't think he has fallen for your pretty faces. He has as much need for you as for yesteryear's macaroni. It's just that he fears delay and is anxious to get on."

"Scandalous!" groaned the priest.

"Sit down here," said the lady, making room for the girls at her side. "We'll be warmer this way."

Talking softly to each other and passing their luggage from hand to hand, the girls climbed into the coach, greeted the passengers, thanked Andersen shyly, took their seats and lapsed into silence. A smell of goat cheese and mint filled the coach. Dark though it was, Andersen could dimly discern the glimmer of cheap stones in the girls' earrings.

When the wheels of the coach were again crunching against the road, the girls began to whisper.

"The girls wish to know if you, Signor, are a foreign prince in disguise, or an ordinary traveller," said the lady in the black cloak. Andersen could almost see her smiling in the darkness.

"I am a fortune-teller," replied Andersen without thinking. "I can tell the future and see in the dark. But don't think me a charlatan. If you wish, think of me as a poor prince from the land where Hamlet once lived."

"And pray, what can you see in such darkness?" asked one of the girls in surprise.

"You, for example," answered Andersen. "I can see you so distinctly that your loveliness fills my heart with admiration."

As he said this he felt cold in the face, and knew that the state he generally experienced when he was about to conceive a poem or a story had come upon him. It brought with it a faint trepidation, a spontaneous flow of words, flashes of poetic images and a sweet awareness of one's powers over the human heart. It was as though the lid of an old magic casket, filled with inexpressed thoughts, long-dormant feelings and with all the charming things of earth, its flowers, colours, sounds, fragrant breezes, the open sea, the murmur of woods, love's longings, and the sweet prattle of babies, had suddenly burst open.

Andersen did not know what to call this state. Some considered it to be inspiration, others a trance, still others the gift of improvisation.

"I was dozing when your voices broke the stillness of the night," Andersen continued calmly after a pause. "My hearing you talk and now my seeing you has been enough, my dear young ladies, for me to read your characters and, even more than that, to admire you, as passing sisters in the night. And though the night is very dark I can see all your faces as well as by daylight. I am looking at one of you now; the one who has fluffy hair. You're a joy-loving creature and so excessively fond of pets that even the wild thrushes sit on your shoulder when you tend the plants in the garden."

"Nicolina, that's surely you he's describing," put in one of the girls in a loud whisper.

"You have a warm and tender heart, Nicolina," Andersen went on in the same calm voice. "If your lover were in trouble you would hurry to his rescue at once even if it meant walking thousands of miles across mountains or arid deserts. Am I right?"

"Yes, I would do that," Nicolina murmured softly, "since you think so."

"What are your names?" asked Andersen.

"Nicolina, Maria and Anna," came the eager voice of one of them.

"As to you, Maria, I regret that my command of Italian is too poor to do justice to your beauty. But while still young, I promised the god of poetry that I would always sing the praises of beauty."

"Scandalous!" the priest muttered in an undertone. "A tarantula has bitten him and he's gone mad!"

"Women of true beauty are almost always of a reserved nature. They have their great secret passions which light up their faces from within. This is true of you, Maria. The fate of such women is often uncommon. They are either very unhappy or very happy."

"Have you ever met such women?" asked the lady passenger.

"I see two of them now before me. They are you, Signora, and Maria, the girl sitting at your side."

"I hope you are not making fun of us," said the lady, and added in an undertone, "it would be far too cruel to this beautiful girl—and to me."

"I have never been more in earnest in all my life, Signora."

"Please, tell me, Signor, shall I be happy or unhappy?" asked Maria after a pause.

"Happiness will not come easy to you, Maria. You want too much from life for a simple peasant lass. But I may tell you this—you will find a man worthy of your proud heart. And I am certain that your chosen one will be a remarkable person. He may be a painter, a poet or a fighter for the freedom of Italy. He may be a simple shepherd or a sailor but a man with a big heart. Who he will be, after all, makes little difference."

"Signor," Maria began shyly, "I cannot see you in the dark and that makes me bold enough to ask you a question. What if such a man as you describe has already taken possession of my heart? And I have seen him only a few times. I do not even know where he may be now."

"Seek him!" cried Andersen. "Find him and he will love you."

"Maria!" Anna cried joyfully. "So, you've fallen in love with that young artist from Verona?"

"Hush!" Maria cried.

"Verona is not so very big, you're sure to find him there," said the lady. "My name is Elena Guiccioli. Try to remember it. I live in Verona where anybody you ask will point out my house to you. And you shall live under my roof until the fates will bring you and your young man together."

Maria found Elena Guiccioli's hand in the dark and pressed it to her burning cheek.

All were silent when Andersen noticed that the green star no longer shone; it had vanished behind the earth's rim which meant that the night was on the wane.

"Why don't you tell me my fortune now, Signor," said Anna.

"You shall be the mother of a large family," Andersen replied with assurance. "Your children will queue up for their jug of milk. And you will spend much time every morning washing and combing them. But your future husband will help you."

"Don't tell me it'll be Pietro?" said Anna. "That big lout, I've no use for him."

"And you will yet spend more time in kissing the sparkling eyes of your little boys and girls full of the eagerness to know everything."

"To think that I should have to listen to such scandalous nonsense in the Pope's own country!" the priest said irascibly. But no one paid the least attention.

Again the girls' whisperings, intermingled with little giggles, filled the coach. At last Maria, mustering up courage, said: "And now, Signor, since we haven't the gift of seeing in the dark and reading people's minds, please tell us something about yourself."

"I'm a wandering minstrel," replied Andersen. "I am rather young. I have thick wavy hair, a darkly tanned face, and blue, laughing eyes. I haven't a care in the world, nor am I in love. It is a hobby of mine to make people small gifts and to commit little follies."

"What sort of follies?"

"Well, last summer, for example, I was in Jutland, staying at the home of a forester I knew. One day while roaming in the woods I came to a clearing with hosts of mushrooms. That very day I went back to the woods and placed under each mushroom a little gift, such as a sweet in a silver wrapper, a date, a tiny nosegay or a thimble tied with a silk ribbon. Next morning I took the forester's seven-year-old daughter to the woods and imagine her delight at the discovery of the little gifts under the mushrooms in the clearing. Everything I had placed the day before was there—except the date, evidently picked up by a crow. And I assured the child that the gifts were left under the mushrooms by the little goblins."

"You have deceived an innocent child, Signor," said the priest indignantly. "That is a great sin!"

"It was no deception. The child, I am certain, will remember my little prank for the rest of her life. And I may assure you that she will not grow hard of heart so easily as others who have not been delighted thus in their childhood. Besides, I would have the Reverend gentleman know that I'm not in the habit of listening to undeserved rebukes."

The coach came to an abrupt halt and the girls sat motionless as though under a spell. Elena Guiccioli's silent head was bowed.

"Hey, beauties, wake up, we've arrived!" called the coachman.

Exchanging a few words in undertones, the girls rose. Andersen felt two strong, supple arms clasp him around his neck and ardent lips were pressed to his own.

"Thank you!" said the lips, and Andersen recognized Maria's voice.

Nicolina thanked him, too. Her kiss was gentle and tender and he felt her hair brush against his cheek. Anna's was a real smack.

The girls jumped to the ground and the coach rolled away along the flagged road. Andersen looked out of the window, but could see nothing except the black tops of the trees against a sky going slightly green before dawn.

Verona, Andersen found, was a city of magnificent architecture. The stately façades of its buildings vied with each other in beauty and the harmonious lines brought peace to the heart. But there was no peace in Andersen's heart.

The evening found him in a narrow street leading up to a fort in front of the ancient palace of the Guiccioli. He rang the bell. And Elena Guiccioli herself opened the door. She wore a green velvet dress clinging to her slender form. It made her eyes seem as green as those of a Valkyrie, and wonderfully beautiful. She stretched both her hands out to him, and clasping his own broad palms in her cool fingers led him with retreating steps into a small hall.

"I have longed for you to come," she said simply.

At these words Andersen turned deathly pale. He had been thinking of nothing but her all day long with repressed emotion. He knew he was capable of loving a woman to distraction, loving every word she uttered, every eyelash that fell from her lids, every speck of dust upon her gown. But he also knew that if he let such love possess him it would burst his heart. With a thousand joys it would bring a thousand torments, with its smiles would come tears. He will have no strength to endure all of love's diverse and unexpected moods. May it not rob him of the power to write his wonderful fairy-tales? What would his life be worth then?

All the same his love could not be other than unrequited. He knew that from experience. Such women like Elena Guiccioli were capricious. One sad day she will surely realize how unattractive he was. Now he was even repugnant to himself. How often he felt mocking looks cast behind his back and his gait would stiffen, he would stumble and pray that the earth would swallow him up.

"Eternal love glorified by the poets exists only in our imagination," he tried to assure himself. "I think I can write about love much better than experience it in real life."

He came to Elena Guiccioli with the firm resolve never to see her again. But could he tell her that when not a word had passed between them and they had set eyes on each other only the evening before in the coach which took them to Verona.

Andersen paused in the doorway, his eyes wandering about the room. In one of the corners, illumined by the candelabrum, his gaze rested on the white marble head of Diana with a face which seemed to pale from the effect of its own beauty.

"Tell me who has made your features immortal in the image of Diana?" asked Andersen.

"Canova," replied Guiccioli and dropped her eyes. Andersen felt that she had divined his most secret thoughts.

"I have come to pay my respects to you," he muttered in husky tones. "Then I shall flee from Verona."

"I have found out who you are," said Elena Guiccioli, her eyes looking into his. "You are Hans Christian Andersen, a poet and the famous writer of fairy-tales. But it seems you are afraid of living a fairy-tale in life. You have not the courage even for a brief love."

"I haven't," Andersen admitted.

"Then, my wandering poet," she said sadly, putting her hand on Andersen's shoulder, "you may flee. And may there be laughter in your eyes always. Do not think of me. But if ever you come to suffer, or if infirmity, poverty or disease overtake you, say but one word, and, like Nicolina, I shall hurry to comfort you, even if I have to walk thousands of miles across mountains or arid deserts."

She dropped into a chair and buried her face in her hands. The candles sputtered in the candelabra. Andersen caught sight of a glistening tear between Elena's fingers. It dropped and slowly rolled down the velvet of her dress. He rushed to her side, fell on his knees and pressed his face against her warm, delicately shaped legs. She took his head in between her hands, bent down and kissed him on the lips.

A second tear dropped on to his face and he tasted its salt.

"Go!" she muttered softly. "And may the gods be good to you."

He rose, took his hat and hastily went out. Verona's streets were filled with the ringing of the evening bells.

They never met again, but never ceased to think of each other.

And this is what Andersen told a young writer some time before his death: "I have paid a great price for my fairy-tales, a terrible price. For their sake I have renounced personal happiness and have let slip the time of life when imagination, despite all its power and splendour, must give place to reality. You, my friend, use your imagination to make others happy, and yourself too."

A BOOK OF BIOGRAPHICAL SKETCHES

Perhaps some ten years ago I began to plan a book containing a series of biographical sketches which I thought would be very interesting but difficult to write. Such sketches must be brief but striking. I started drawing up a list of the remarkable personalities which would go into the book.

Apart from biographies of famous people, I wished to include a number of brief pen portraits of various interesting persons I had met at one time or another. The latter had never achieved fame or won homage, but were no less worthy of both. That they had led obscure lives and left no trace of their existence is merely one of the vagaries of fortune. For the most part they were unselfish and ardent idealists inspired by some single purpose.

One of these was Captain Olenin-Volgar, a man who had led quite a fabulous life. He was brought up in a family of musicians and studied singing in Italy. Seized by a desire to travel on foot through Europe he dropped his music lessons and roamed through Italy, France and

Spain as a street-singer, singing the popular songs of these countries to the accompaniment of the guitar.

I made Olenin-Volgar's acquaintance in 1924, in the office of a Moscow newspaper. He was then a lean old man of slight build and he wore the uniform of a river captain. One day after working hours we begged him to sing. His voice rang young and his performance was splendid in every way. Fascinated, we listened to Italian songs which flowed with remarkable ease, to the jerky rhythms of Basque melodies, and to the martial strains of the *Marseillaise*, bringing with it the trumpet-calls and smoke of battle-fields.

After his wanderings through Europe, Olenin-Volgar became a seaman, qualified for a pilot and sailed the length and breadth of the Mediterranean over and over again. Later, on returning to Russia, he became captain of a Volga passenger boat. At the time I got acquainted with him he was sailing from Moscow to Nizhni-Novgorod and back.

He was the first to risk navigating a large Volga passenger steamer through the old, narrow sluices of the Moskva River, which all his colleagues claimed was impossible. And he was also the first to submit a project for straightening the Moskva river-bed near the notorious Marchugi country where the river twisted. At this point in the river there were so many bends that even to see them on a map was enough to make one's head reel.

Captain Olenin-Volgar had written many interesting articles on the rivers of Russia—articles now lost and forgotten. He knew all the dangerous places and shoals in dozens of Russian rivers, and he had quite simple, effective schemes for improving navigation along these rivers.

His spare time he spent translating Dante's *Divine Comedy* into Russian.

He was an upright, generous-hearted person who loved adventure and respected all people as equals regardless of their standing in life. They were "good folk on this good earth" serving the cause of the people.

The curator of a Regional Museum in a little town of Central Russia was another simple-hearted and dear acquaintance of mine. The museum in which my friend worked was housed in a very old building. He had nobody to help him look after the museum except his wife. Apart from taking care of the exhibits and the files, these two persons did all the repairs and chores themselves, even bringing in supplies of firewood for the winter.

Once I found the couple strangely engaged. They were picking up every little stone and bit of chipped brick they could find in the street around the museum and carrying these into the back-yard. It appeared that the street boys had broken a window in the museum and they were clearing the street of missiles.

Every item in the museum—from a sample of old lace and a rare specimen of 14th-century building brick to bits of peat and a stuffed Argentine water-rat, brought for breeding purposes to the surrounding bogs—had been studied and described in detail by the curator.

Always unobtrusive, speaking in undertones and often coughing to hide his embarrassment, he would beam all over whenever he showed to visitors the museum's pride: a painting by Perepletchikov he had managed to pick up in a closed-down monastery. It was a splendid landscape—a view opening from the deep embrasure of a window—of an evening in the north with young drowsy birches and the tinfoil water of a small lake.

The curator found his work difficult. He was not always appreciated. But he went about his duties conscientiously, giving no trouble to anyone. And even if his museum was not of any great benefit to society, was not his own way of living an inspiring example of devotion to a purpose, modesty and regional patriotism to the people around him?

Quite recently I came across the list of the personalities which were to go into the book of biographical sketches I planned. The list is long and it contains many writers. I shall pick out a few names at random.

Beside the name of each writer I jotted down brief and disjointed notes, mostly of the sentiments aroused in me by these writers. I should like to reproduce some of these notes here.

CHEKHOV

The many journals left to us by Chekhov can claim a place all their own in literature. He rarely, however, drew upon the matter contained in them for his stories.

There are also the journals of Ilya Ilf, Alphonse Daudet, diaries by Lev Tolstoi, the Goncourt brothers, the French writer Renard and many others.

These have the legitimate right to be classed as an independent *genre* in literature. But, contrary to the views of many writers, I think them to be practically of no use as sources of material and inspiration.

For some time I kept a journal myself. But every time I tried to select some interesting entry out of it and incorporate it in the story or novel I happened to be working on at the time, it somehow did not fit in and hung loose and disjointed.

Perhaps the only way to account for this is that the "material" stored up subconsciously by our memory is far more important than notes made at any time of our lives. That which we do not trust to our memory but make a point of jotting down will rarely prove of use. It is memory which is the most reliable filter of material, an intricate sieve, discarding the rubbish we do not need and leaving grains of gold for us to pick out and use.

Chekhov had been a doctor before he became a writer. It is a good idea, I think, for a writer to be engaged for a while in some non-literary profession.

Chekhov's being a doctor, in addition to helping him to learn much about people, also affected his style, making his prose analytical, precise and as incisive as a scalpel. Some of his stories (for example, "Ward No. 6," "Dull Story," "The Grasshopper") are really the skilfully written and extended case-histories of a psychoanalyst.

Compactness and terseness are characteristic of Chekhov's prose. "Delete everything superfluous, all redundant words and hackneyed expressions," Chekhov used to say, "and strive to give a musical quality to each sentence." There were, by the way, many words of foreign origin that Chekhov had an aversion for and avoided using. Some of these were *аппетит* (appetite), *флирт* (flirt), *идеал* (ideal), *диск* (disk), *экран* (screen).

Chekhov spent much of his life in trying to better himself. He said that bit by bit he fought to eradicate all elements in his nature which made him a slave to things. And a close chronological examination of his photographs from his youth to the last years of his life will show the gradual disappearance of all vestiges of the middle class from his appearance, his face growing more serene and significant, his attire attaining the true elegance of simplicity.

There is a little corner in our land which is dear to all—Chekhov's house in Yalta. For my generation thoughts of this house recall our young days and bring to memory the loving voice of its custodian, Maria Pavlovna, Chekhov's sister, better known as Chekhov's dear Masha.

It was in 1949 that I last visited the house at Yalta and sat with Maria Pavlovna on its terrace. Masses of sweet-smelling white blossoms hid Yalta and the sea from view. Maria Pavlovna told me that they had been planted by Chekhov himself. She remembered that he had called them by some fancy name but the name itself had escaped her memory. Maria Pavlovna had a way of speaking of her brother as though he were still alive and had merely absented himself for a while from the house— on a visit to Moscow or Nice.

I plucked a camellia in Chekhov's garden and gave it to a little girl who had come along with me to visit Maria Pavlovna. But the thoughtless little creature dropped the flower into a mountain stream from a bridge we were passing and it was carried away to the sea. I would have scolded her had I not felt that day that Chekhov might appear in our midst at any moment and he certainly would not approve of my chiding a little shy, grey-eyed girl for such a trifle as dropping a camellia picked in his garden into the water.

ALEXANDER BLOK

Among Blok's little-known poems there is one called "The Warm Night Clothed the Islands." In it there is a line, lingering and sweet, bringing back the loveliness of our long-lost youth—*Vesna moyei mechty dalekoi.** The Russian words are exquisite and the line divine. What is true of this line, is true of all of Blok's poetry.

On my many trips to Leningrad I always longed to walk (walk and not ride by bus or tram) all the way to the Pryazhka and to find the house where Blok had lived and died.

I did set out once but only to lose my way among the deserted streets and slimy canals of this out-of-the-way

* Spring of my early dreams.—*Tr.*

district and in a by-street came across a house which had once been occupied not by Blok but by Dostoyevsky. It was a faded brick building with a memorial tablet on its front side.

Some time ago, however, on the embankment of the Pryazhka, I finally found the house where Blok had lived. The black river was strewn with the shrivelled leaves of autumn. Beyond it extended the city's bustling wharves and shipyards with clouds of smoke rolling over them and rising into the pale evening sky. But the river itself was tranquil and desolate like that of a provincial town.

A strange haven for a poet like Blok! I wondered—did Blok wish to find in this quiet neighbourhood, not far from the sea, the peace that a heart in turmoil seeks?

GUY DE MAUPASSANT

"His life was a sealed book to us."
RENARD

When he lived on the Riviera, Maupassant owned a yacht which he named *Bel ami*. It was aboard this yacht that he had written *Sur l'eau*, one of his most pessimistic and powerful stories.

There were two sailors on the yacht—the elder called Bernard—who witnessed the great French writer struggle through the last painful months of his life and tried their utmost to be as cheerful and understanding as possible. Never by word or gesture did they betray the alarm they felt for the writer's life. With anguished hearts they watched him being driven to insanity not so much by the thoughts that whirled in his mind as by the terrific headaches that gave him no peace.

When Maupassant died the sailors, who perhaps knew better that many others that Maupassant had a proud and sensitive heart, did not wish his yacht to pass into the hands of a stranger. And so in a clumsy scrawl they wrote a letter to a French newspaper, and made vain appeals to Maupassant's friends as well as to all writers of France to buy the yacht. Though poverty weighed heavily on them they kept the yacht in their care as long as they could. Finally they sold it to Count Barthélemy, a wealthy idler.

When Bernard was dying he said to his friends: "I was not a bad sailor, after all."

In these simple words was summed up a life nobly lived. They may also be applied to Maupassant's own life and work.

Maupassant's career as a writer was amazingly mercurial. "I entered literary life like a meteor," he said, "and I shall leave it like lightning."

An impartial observer of human lechery, an anatomist who called life "the writer's clinic," Maupassant towards the end of his days recognized the value of a wholesome life and unsullied love.

Even in his last days, when he could feel the effects of an insidious disease on his brain, we are told that he deeply regretted having turned aside from the nobler aspects of life and let himself be completely absorbed by its vanities.

Had he, the helmsman, guided his fellow creatures to any definite goal? What promise of fulfilment had he held out to them? None. Now he knew that had there been room for compassion in his writings, humanity would have remembered him with greater gratitude.

He craved for affection like a neglected child, frowning and shrinking. Love, he realized, was not lust but sacrifice of self, deep joy and poetic delight. But this realization came too late and to his lot fell only regrets and pangs of conscience.

He had scoffed at love and mocked at those who loved him. When Mlle Bashkirtseva, the young Russian painter, had fallen in love with him, he reciprocated by a derisive and somewhat coquettish correspondence merely to tickle his masculine vanity.

Yet another true love he had slighted, and regretted even more. He recalled the little Parisian grisette. Her love had but served as subject-matter for one of Paul Bourget's stories. How dared that drawing-room psychologist tamper so unabashedly with real human tragedy—Maupassant now thought with indignation. But it was really he, Maupassant, who was to blame for it all. And there was nothing to be done now when he no longer had the strength to fight the disease—he could even hear the crackling of the sharp little crystals piercing the interstices of his brain.

The grisette—so lovely and so innocent! She had been reading his stories and after setting eyes on Maupassant but once had loved him, loved him with all the youthful ardour of her heart, a heart as pure and guileless as her sparkling eyes.

Naive creature—she discovered that Maupassant was a bachelor and took it into her head that she and no other was fit to be his mate, his wife, his servant.

She was poor and badly dressed and so she starved for a whole year, putting by every centime she could, to buy herself the elegant clothes in which she wished to appear before Maupassant.

At last the garments were ready. She awoke early in the morning when Paris was still asleep, wrapped in the mist of dreams, and the first rays of the rising sun were breaking. This was the only hour of the day when the singing of the birds in the linden boulevards was audible in the city.

After bathing herself in cold water, slowly and gently, with the homage due to things of fragile and fragrant beauty, she began putting on the sheer stockings, the tiny glittering slippers and finally her costly gown. On beholding her image in the mirror, she could hardly believe her eyes. She saw a slender and beautiful young woman, beaming with joy and excitement, with eyes that were dark pools of love and a mouth delicately moulded and pink. Now she would present herself to Maupassant and make a full confession.

A few hours later found her ringing the bell at the gate of the summer residence near Paris where Maupassant lived. She was let in by one of the writer's friends, a voluptuary and shameless cynic. Laughing, his eyes greedily taking in the curves of her young body, he told her that Monsieur Maupassant had gone with his mistress to spend a few days in Etretat.

The girl turned hastily on her heel, and walked away clasping the railing with her small gloved hand.

Maupassant's friend hurried after her, got her into a carriage and drove her to Paris. She wept bitterly, even spoke of revenge and that very night gave herself to him in a fit of despair. A year later found her a notorious courtesan in Paris.

When the story was related to Maupassant by his friend it did not occur to him then that the man had behaved like a cad and that the least he could do was to strike him across the face. Instead he found it quite amusing; not a bad subject for a story, he had thought.

What a tragedy that he was now powerless to turn the wheels of time back to the day when the little shop girl stood at the gate of his home like sweet-smelling spring and trustfully proffered her heart! He did not even know her name. But now she was dear to him and he thought of all the caressing names he could call her.

Writhing with pain, he was ready to kiss the ground she walked on and beg forgiveness—he, the great and haughty Maupassant. But it was all in vain. The story had merely served as an excuse for Bourget to expatiate on the vagaries of the human heart.

The vagaries of the heart!—the girl's love for him was a noble passion, the holy of holies in our imperfect world. He could write about it a marvellous story, were it not for the poisons in his brain, eating into it, sapping his power to think and live.

MAXIM GORKY

Reams have already been written about Maxim Gorky. And it would be presumptuous on my part to add but a single line were it not for the inexhaustible wealth of his personality.

The influence that Gorky has exercised over each of us is perhaps greater than that of any single writer. So much so that his presence is felt in our midst all the time and his name is ready off our lips.

To me Gorky is Russia and just as I can't imagine Russia without the Volga I can't imagine it without Gorky.

Gorky stands for all that is noblest in the genius of the Russian people. He is one of the great landmarks of our revolutionary age. He loved and knew Russia as few people did. He exerted tremendous effort and grudged no time to spot and develop talent and in this way more than any other writer of his time helped to father Soviet literature. There was nothing in the land too trifling to command his attention. His interests extended to spheres far removed from literature and upon them, too, he left the mark of his talent.

When I first met Gorky I was struck by the grace of his person. Even his stoop and the harsh notes of his Volga accent did not diminish this effect. His personality had evidently reached that stage of spiritual fulfilment when inner integrity sets its stamp on the appearance, on gestures, manner of speaking and even dress.

His was a grace combined with great strength of character. It was there in the movement of his broad hands, in the intentness of his gaze, in his gait and in the artistic carelessness with which he wore his loose-fitting garments.

The following incident related to me by a writer who was Gorky's guest in his Crimean home in Tesseli impressed me so much that it helped me to form a mental picture of the great writer.

Early one morning this writer awoke and as he looked out of the window he saw a violent storm raging over the sea. The southern wind whistled in the gardens and rattled the weather-vanes.

Some distance away from the house he caught sight of Gorky standing in front of a majestic poplar. Leaning on his walking stick, he was looking up at the tree, whose thick crown of foliage swayed and filled the air with a murmuring, loud as the strains of a huge organ. For a long time Gorky stood bare-headed, staring up at the tree. Then he muttered something to himself and went farther into the garden, but not without stopping a few times to look back at the poplar.

At supper the writer begged Gorky to tell him what he had said while gazing at the tree.

"So, you've been spying on me," said Gorky laughing. "I don't mind telling you. I said: 'What might!' "

I remember one summer day paying a visit to Gorky in his countryhouse not far from Moscow. Foamy clouds drifted in the sky and the landscape across the Moskva River folded into green, rolling hills with shadows flitting here and there. A warm breeze swept through the rooms of the house.

Gorky began discussing *Colchis,* a novel of mine which had just been published. The scene of the novel was laid in the subtropics and Gorky spoke to me as though I was an authority on life in that part of the country. That embarrassed me and I was happy when we drifted into an argument about the prevalence of malaria among dogs. Gorky, who at first claimed that dogs were never affected by the disease, soon admitted that he was wrong, turning the whole argument into a joke. He spoke in a rich and vivid language which to most of us now is a lost gift.

It was during that visit that I told Gorky about a book called *The Ice-Sheet* by Captain Garnet, who had at one time been our Marines' representative in Japan. It was there that he had written his book and set it in type himself, because he could not find a Japanese compositor who knew Russian. He had printed only five hundred copies on thin Japanese paper, and I was lucky enough to have one of these.

In this book Captain Garnet evolves a rather amusing theory. I shall not go into details about it for it would require too much space. Briefly, it concerns the possibility of Europe reverting to the subtropical climate of the Miocene period when dense forests of magnolia and cypress-trees grew along the shores of the Bay of Finland and even on Spitsbergen. To bring back the Miocene period and usher in a golden age in the vegetation of Europe it was necessary to melt the ice sheet of Greenland. And since this was utterly impossible, Captain Garnet's theory, though built up on extremely convincing arguments, was not very tenable. Perhaps now, with the discovery of atomic energy, there is a greater possibility of applying the theory.

As I gave Gorky a bare outline of Garnet's theory, he kept drumming on the table with his fingers and it seemed to me that he was listening merely out of politeness.

It proved, however, that he was quite carried away by the ideas propounded in the book and, greatly animated, begged me to send him my copy of it so that he could have it reprinted in Russia. Garnet's well-founded arguments and surmises filled Gorky with wonder at the ingenuity of the human mind which, he claimed, was manifesting itself more forcefully and universally day by day.

Death prevented Maxim Gorky from keeping his promise in regard to this interesting book.

VICTOR HUGO

In the English Channel, on the Island of Jersey, where Victor Hugo had lived in exile, a monument to him was erected. It stands in wild country on a high cliff overlooking the ocean.

The pedestal, no more than a foot or so in height, with the grass growing tall and thick around it, is hidden from view so that the feet of the statue seem to be planted on the ground. In a fluttering cloak, holding his hat down on his head with one hand and his back bowed, Victor Hugo is shown struggling fearlessly against a boisterous ocean gale. Not far from the statue is the rock where the sailor Jelliot from *The Toilers of the Sea* met his death.

All around as far as the eye can reach stretches the roaring ocean. Swelling billows break on the reefs, thrashing and swaying the seaweeds and smashing into the caves.

In foggy weather, the shrill lighthouse sirens cut through the air. Beacon-lights can be seen rocking on the surface of the water, and from time to time are submerged by the huge waves beating against the shores of the island.

Every year on the anniversary of Victor Hugo's death

the inhabitants of Jersey choose the prettiest girl on the island to place a few mistletoe twigs at the foot of the statue. According to traditional belief this plant, which has firm, oval-shaped, green leaves, brings happiness to the living and long remembrance to the dead.

The belief is justified; and Victor Hugo's rebellious spirit still hovers over France.

Victor Hugo was volcanic, ardent, and fiery-spirited. He exaggerated everything he saw and wrote. Life to him spelled great passions. With them he was at home and he wrote about them in forceful elevated language which may be likened to an orchestra of wind instruments with him as its talented conductor. In it sounded the jubilant blasts of the trumpets, the roar of the kettledrums, the piercing and melancholy notes of the flutes, the high-pitched sounds of the hautboys. The powerful notes of this orchestra, like the thundering of ocean breakers, shook the world, and made faint hearts shudder. Nor had he any compassion for these hearts. His longing to imbue all humanity with the wrath against injustice, with the burning passions, and above all the devotion to liberty which he himself felt, knew no bounds.

In Victor Hugo liberty found its true champion, its great mouthpiece, its herald and troubadour, one who seemed to be calling: "To arms, citizens, to arms!"

Like a hurricane he burst upon an age, at once classical and dull, bringing torrents of rain, whirling leaves, thunder-clouds, the scent of sweet flowers, as well as the smell of gunpowder and hosts of flying cockades.

The spirit he brought to that age is called Romanticism. It set into motion the stagnant waters of Europe and brought to the continent the breath of great and noble dreams.

I was greatly impressed and charmed by Victor Hugo while still a child after I had read *Les Misérables* five times in succession. I would finish the book and that same day begin reading it again. I had then got hold of a map of Paris and marked all the places where the action of the novel takes place. I felt as though I myself was involved in the action and to this day Jean Valjean, Cozette and Gavroche are as dear to me as any childhood friends.

Victor Hugo had made me love Paris as ardently as one loves the cities of one's own Motherland. And as the years went by that love for the city I've never seen grew deeper. To Victor Hugo's description of Paris were added those of Balzac, Maupassant, Dumas, Flaubert, Zola, Jules Vallès, Anatole France, Romain Rolland, Daudet, Villon, Rimbaud, Mérimée, Stendhal, Barbusse and Béranger.

I had a note-book full of poems I collected about Paris. To my regret I lost it, but many of the verses I remember by heart. They were all different, some pompous, others simple.

> *You will come to a fairy-tale city,*
> *Blessed in prayers by centuries long,*
> *And you'll feel your weariness lifting*
> *And your spirit forgetting its wrongs.*
>
> *Then you'll walk in the Luxembourg gardens,*
> *Past the fountains, down paths far away,*
> *In the shadow of spreading platans,*
> *Like Mimi in the book by Murger.*

Thus it was Victor Hugo who inspired many of us with our first love for Paris, and we are grateful to him for it, especially those of us who were never fortunate enough to see that wonderful city.

MIKHAIL PRISHVIN

If it were in Nature's power to feel gratitude to one of her most devoted singers, that gratitude would be best deserved by Mikhail Prishvin.

The name by which he is known to city people is Mikhail Mikhailovich Prishvin, but in those places where he felt most at home—in the huts of foresters, in mist-enveloped floodlands, out in the fields under the overcast or starry sky, he was called simply and loving-ly "Mikhalich." It even pained these country people to see him leave—when necessity called for it—for towns with nothing except the swallows nestling under the iron roofs to remind him of the open spaces.

Prishvin's life is an example of one who cared little for trivialities or conventions and lived, as he said him-self, according to the "dictates of the heart." There is indeed much wisdom in such a way of life. One who lives thus and is in harmony with his spirit is to my mind ever a creator, an enricher and an artist.

It is hard to say what Prishvin would have accom-plished had he remained in the humble calling of an agriculturist which he was by education. But as a writer he has been able to help millions of people delight in the subtle and lucid poetry of the world of Russian nature which he re-created for them in his books. All of his keen powers of observation he focused upon nature, drinking in her magic beauty and constantly enriching it by thought and reflection.

A close reading of all that Prishvin has ever written makes it obvious that he tells but a hundredth part of what he saw and knew.

Prishvin was the kind of writer who needed more than a lifetime to fulfil himself, the kind that could write a whole poem about a single autumn leaf dropping from a tree. And so many of these leaves fall bearing away the writer's unuttered thoughts, thoughts which Prishvin had said may drop as effortlessly upon the world as these self-same leaves.

It was in the ancient Russian town of Yelets that Prishvin was born. Curiously, this town was also the birthplace of Ivan Bunin, another writer who was a master of Nature and who, like Prishvin, was able to suggest an affinity between the moods of Nature and the emotional states of man.

Perhaps it is the fact that the countryside around the old town of Yelets has the charm of being typically Russian—unobtrusive and sparing, even severe, that accounts for this. It is these qualities in the landscape that explain the sharpness of Prishvin's vision; when Nature's outlines are simple and scant, they are more easily grasped by the mind and impress themselves more vividly upon the imagination.

Unobtrusive effects in Nature may have a deeper appeal than riotous colours, blazing sunsets, skies swarming with stars, the luxuriant vegetation of the tropics with its wealth of foliage and flowers.

It is difficult to write about Prishvin. I would recommend passages from his stories to be copied out and re-read to discover new beauties in every line. Reading Prishvin's books is a wonderful experience. It is like going down hardly perceptible paths leading to trackless forests with babbling brooks and sweet-smelling grass. And as you do this you enter into the versatile thoughts and moods of his pure mind and heart.

Prishvin would say that he was a poet sacrificed on the altar of prose. But he was mistaken. His prose is richer in the essence of true poetry than many verses and long poems.

Writing was to him, as he put it himself, "the joy of constantly making new discoveries." Hence the freshness of his style. He is able to exercise an amazing power over his readers. "He's a wizard, he keeps you under a spell," I've heard readers say about his books.

That is the peculiar Prishvin charm, a charm often attributed to writers of fairy-tales. But Prishvin is not a writer of fairy-tales. He is a man of the soil, of "damp mother-earth," a keen observer of life and nature. The great secret of Prishvin's power as a writer is his ability to read great meaning into what appear to be trifling things. Thus, he lifts the veil of tedium from the commonplace and reveals the romance, beauty and depth hidden away beneath it, making whatever he touches shine with poetic radiance like bedewed grass.

I take one of Prishvin's books, open it and read:

"The night passed beneath a full, clear moon. And the morning brought the first light frost. But for the unfrozen pools everything gleamed a silvery white. When the sun rose and spread its warmth over the soil, the trees and shrubs were so bathed with dew and the boughs of the fir-trees shone forth in such glory against the black of the woods that all the jewels of the earth would have hardly sufficed to replace Nature's handiwork."

This passage, unaffected and precise, is full of immortal poetry.

Gorky said that Prishvin possessed "the consummate faculty of imparting an almost physical reality to simple word combinations."

But there is more that can be said about Prishvin's language. He uses the rich vocabulary of the simple people, a vocabulary with its roots deep in the soil, in labour processes, in the directness and wisdom of the national character.

Prishvin's feeling for words is amazing. It is said of his words that they bloom and sparkle, bringing to his pages the rustling of grass, the gurgling of water, the twittering of the birds, the tinkling of young ice, and slowly but surely possess our minds as the stars possess the heavens above us.

His extensive knowledge of whatever he writes accounts for much of the uncanny hold that Prishvin's prose has on his reader. Knowledge of the sciences can be of great help to the poet. I think the poet could do better justice to the starry sky—a favourite theme with poets—if he knew more about astronomy. He would be able to write more expressively of the properties of the stars and the movements of the constellations—and more concretely.

There are many examples when even a little knowledge will quicken our sense of appreciation. All of us, I am certain, have had some experiences along these lines.

In my own case I can cite an example when but a single line in one of Prishvin's stories explained to me the reason for a certain phenomenon which I had till then regarded as purely incidental. It did more than that—it revealed its true charm to me.

I had for a long time noticed that in the flood meadows bordering on the Oka flowers grew in flaming belts. You get a particularly good view of the country cut up by these belts from the small U-2 plane which sprinkles the marshes with insecticide. I was puzzled, of course, why the flowers should grow in long belts. But being at a loss to explain the reason, did not rack my brains too much over it.

In Prishvin's book *Seasons of the Year* I found the explanation I needed. It was there in a single line—in a small passage entitled "Rivers of Flowers." "Where the spring torrents flowed now are rivers of flowers," it read. And at once I understood that the belts of flowers grew there where the spring torrents had passed and fertilized the land, forming a sort of flower map of spring waters.

Some distance from Moscow flows the Dubna. You will find it on the map. It is an old river, its banks now inhabited for over a thousand years. It flows peacefully through groves overgrown with hop, past rolling blue hills and fields and old Russian towns and villages such as Dmitrov, Verbilki, Taldom. Thousands of people have visited its banks, among them writers, artists and poets. Yet no one had found anything remarkable about this river, anything worthy of their pen or brush. No one had tried to fathom or reveal its beauties.

But Prishvin in his stories made the modest Dubna sparkle in all its glory amidst blue mists and fading sunsets. He rediscovered it for the reader as one of the country's most fascinating rivers, with a life all its own, a landscape all its own, reviving its history and describing the habits of the people who live on its banks.

We have had scientists who wrote about science with the hearts of poets. Among them were the naturalist Timiryazev, the historian Klyuchevsky, the naturalist Kaigorodov, the geologist Fersman, the geographer Obruchev, the zoologist Menzbir, the traveller Arsenyev and the botanist Kozhevnikov who died young yet managed to write a most fascinating book on spring and autumn in plant life.

And we have had writers able to make science an integral part of their work—Melnikov-Pechersky, Aksakov, Gorky, Pinegin and others.

But Prishvin, an amazingly erudite writer, stands in a class by himself, for he was able with great skill to organically and unobtrusively incorporate in his prose his extensive knowledge of ethnography, phenology, botany, zoology, agronomy, meteorology, history, folklore, ornithology, geography, regional history and so on. Knowledge lived in his work, enriched by personal experience and observation. Moreover, Prishvin had the happy quality of seeing in scientific phenomena, both large and small, the highest expression of poetry.

When Prishvin writes about people one imagines that he does so with his eyes slightly screwed up, intent on seeing as deeply as possible into them. And he has been able to penetrate through acquired mannerisms, always eager to get at the bottom of the character he describes, whether the character in question is a lumber-jack, a shoemaker, a hunter or a celebrated scientist.

To probe the armour of his character, to learn his most dearly cherished dream is the writer's task. But it is a difficult task, for a man will conceal a long-cherished dream more than anything else—perhaps for fear of being ridiculed, or worse, sensing the utter indifference of his listener.

Only when he is absolutely certain of sympathy is he likely to trust another with something that is very sacred to him. And Prishvin could always be trusted. Moreover one could rely upon him to take the dreamer's side.

Prishvin's diaries and journals contain many interesting thoughts on literary craftsmanship. Through them all runs the idea that prose must be lucid, simple and as refreshing and poetic as spring. That is exactly what Prishvin's prose is like. The esteem and love he enjoys among Soviet readers are well deserved.

ALEXANDER GREEN

In my school-days, all of us boys avidly read the "Universal Library" pocket editions, printed in small type and having yellow jackets. These little volumes were cheap and that suited us very well. You could buy, for example, a copy of Daudet's *Tartarin* or Hamsun's *Mysterier* for ten kopeks. Dickens' *David Copperfield* or Cervantes' *Don Quixote* for twenty.

The "Universal Library" rarely included Russian writers in its lists. Hence when I bought a copy of a newly printed volume of short stories with the bizarre title *Blue Cascade of Telluri* and saw on the cover that it was by

Alexander Green I never suspected the author to be a Russian.

The book contained several stories. I remember opening the volume at the book-stand where I bought it, and reading a passage at random. This is how it ran:

"There was no more disorderly and yet no more fascinating port town than Liss. The people spoke many languages and the town was like a vagabond who had finally decided to settle down. The houses stood helter-skelter in what may be vaguely termed as streets. There could not be any streets in the conventional meaning of the word in Liss, for the town had sprung up on cracked cliffs and hillsides joined by stairways, bridges and narrow passages.

"The town was immersed in luxuriant tropical vegetation, casting fanlike shadows with the sparkle of ardent female glances among them. Yellow stone, blue shade, fanciful crevices in old walls made up the scene. In some rutted back-yard a sullen, barefooted fellow would be smoking a pipe and repairing a huge boat. Echoes of far-away singing carried across the gulleys. Bazaars spread over piles in tents and under huge umbrellas. A gleam of bare arms, bright-coloured fabrics, the aroma of flowers and herbs filled one with a painful longing for love and love's sweet meetings. As unkempt as a young chimney-sweep, the harbour was cluttered with slumbering rolls of sails to be spread in the morning, and beyond it stretched the green water, the cliffs and the broad ocean. At night the stars blazed with dazzling brilliance and the boats resounded with laughter. That was Liss for you!"

I read on, standing in the shade of one of Kiev's chestnut-trees and could not tear myself away from the story, gripping and fantastic as a dream, until I had finished it.

It filled me with a longing for the spanking wind and the salty smell of brine, for Liss, for its sultry lanes, the sparkling eyes of its women, for the rough yellow gravel of its streets mixed with splinters of sea-shells, and the rosy smoke of clouds rising swiftly up into the blue bowl of the sky.

It was more than a longing that I felt, it was a burning desire to see all that I had read about with my own eyes and to plunge into the carefree, maritime life described by Alexander Green.

Suddenly it occurred to me that bits of the colourful world Green describes were familiar to me. What did Liss remind me of? Of Sevastopol, of course, of that town which had risen from the green waves of the sea to meet the dazzling white sun, and was cut up by shadows as blue as the sky. The merry, whirling life of Sevastopol—it was all there in the pages of Green's book.

When reading Green I came across the following sailor song:

> *There's the Southern Cross shining afar,*
> *Now the compass awakes with the swell.*
> *While the vessels He guards*
> *May God save us as well!*

I did not know then that Green himself wrote songs for his stories.

Sparkling wine, glorious sunshine, care-free joy, invigorating adventure and all that made life sweet filled the pages of Green's stories. His stories were as intoxicating as rare, fragrant gusts of fresh air which sweep you off your feet after the suffocating closeness of the city.

Such was my first acquaintance with Green. When I learned that he was a Russian and that his real name was Alexander Stepanovich Grinevsky, I was not particularly surprised, as I had already begun to associate him with the group of Russian writers who had chosen the Black Sea as the scene for their stories. To this group belonged Eduard Bagritsky, Valentin Katayev and many others.

What did surprise me was how Green who—as I had learned from his autobiography—had been an outcast and a vagabond, a lonely, unhappy man, hard-hit by life, could produce books of such beauty and romance and was able to keep his faith in mankind. In speaking of his attitude to life he used to say that he always saw "silvery clouds above the squalor and filth of the slums."

He might well have applied to himself the words of the French writer Jules Renard: "The land over which sail the most beautiful clouds is my native country."

Had he written nothing else but *Crimson Sails*, a poem in prose, this book would have sufficed to place his name side by side with all great writers who knew how to move the heart and elevate the mind.

Green wrote his books in defence of dreams. We are grateful to him for having been one of our greatest dreamers, for is not the future upon which we set so much store born of man's never-dying faculty to dream and to love?

EDUARD BAGRITSKY

We might as well warn Eduard Bagritsky's biographers that they will have a hard time establishing the facts of his life. The reason for this is that the poet was in the habit of spreading the most fantastic stories about himself. These became so inseparably linked up with his life that it is now impossible to distinguish fact from fiction.

And is it really necessary? No sooner would Bagritsky begin inventing things about himself than he sincerely believed that they had actually happened to him, and made others believe so, too. The stories he told about himself became woven into the texture of his life. It is indeed impossible to think of this poet with his grey, laughing eyes and his musical asthmatic voice, without the strange stories he was fond of relating about himself.

We have all heard about the Levantines, a gay, energetic people, full of the joy of living, who live on the shores of the Aegean Sea. These people are a mixture of various nationalities—Greek, Turk, Arab, Jew, Syrian, Italian.

We have our own "Levantines"—the people inhabiting the shores of the Black Sea. They, too, comprise different nationalities and they, too, bubble over with the joy of living; they are brave, witty and passionately in love with their Black Sea, with the dry sunny weather on its shores, with luscious apricots and melons, with the bustling life of its ports....

Bagritsky was typical of these people. He called to mind now a lazy sailor from a Kherson barge, or a mischievous Odessa lad out to catch birds, now a gallant fighter of Kotovsky's army, or Thyl Uylenspiegel. Add to these diverse traits a selfless devotion to poetry and an amazing knowledge of it, and you will get some idea of this poet's irresistible charm.

I first met Bagritsky by the breakwater in Odessa's harbour. He had then just completed his "Poem about a Water-Melon," which was amazingly lush in feeling and language and brought the splash of the sea-waves to its pages.

With our fishing-lines cast far out into the sea, we waited for bullheads to bite. Black barges with patched sails loaded with mountains of striped water-melons drifted by, tossed back and forth by a violent wind, and now and then dipping deep into the foamy water.

Licking the brine off his lips, Bagritsky began in a breathless, singsong voice to recite his new poem. It was the story of a young girl who finds a water-melon washed on to the shore by the tide. The water-melon with a heart carved on it, as the poet supposes, came from a schooner lost at sea.

> And no one was there to explain it to her,
> 'Twas my heart that she held in her hands. . . .

Bagritsky had a remarkable memory and could recite the verses of almost any poet by heart. Nor did he ever have to be coaxed. A master of recitation, he made the most familiar poems ring new. I have never heard anybody before or after Bagritsky recite so well.

He brought out the music of each word and line with a thrilling and lingering vigour. And whatever he recited whether it was Burns' "John the Barley Corn," Blok's "Donna Anna" or Pushkin's "For the Shores of My Distant Land"—I listened to him with a tingling sensation, a contraction in the throat, a desire to weep.

From the harbour we made our way to a tea-house at the Greek bazaar. There we knew was a chance of getting some saccharine with our tea, as well as a slice of black bread and some *brinza.** And we had not had anything to eat since early morning.

There was an old beggar living in Odessa then who was known as "the terror of the tea-houses." But what made him a terror— for he struck fear into the hearts of all the customers—was the odd manner in which he demanded alms. He never humbled himself, never put out a trembling hand, as other beggars did, or shrilled: "Merciful gentlemen, help a poor beggar!" No! This tall, gaunt, grey-bearded old fellow with bloodshot eyes would stretch himself to his full height and even before crossing the threshold of the tea-house would begin in a thundering voice to shower imprecations on the heads of the customers. And he was so resourceful that he could have

---

* Cheese made of sheep's milk.—*Tr.*

easily put to shame even Jeremiah, the Bible's most dismal prophet.

"Have you a conscience, are you human?!" the old man would shout and proceed to answer his rhetorical question himself in the following manner: "Certainly not, if you can sit there munching bread and gorging yourselves on fat cheese when there stands before you a bent old man who has not had a bite since morning and whose insides feel like an empty tub. Your mothers would rejoice in their graves at not having lived to see what blackguards you've grown up to be. Why do you turn away from me? You aren't deaf, are you? Appease your filthy conscience and help a starving old man!"

And all without exception dug into their pockets and produced what coins they had. Rumours had it that for the money the beggar collected he speculated in salt on the black market.

We were served with steaming tea and what then seemed to us really splendid cheese wrapped in a moist linen cloth. The cheese was so salty that it hurt the gums to eat it.

"Aha!" said Bagritsky ominously when he saw the old man enter the tea-house and begin his harangue. "I think I'll teach him a lesson this time. Just let him come over here."

"And what'll happen?" I asked.

"He'll wish he never came!" answered Bagritsky. "Wait and see!"

The beggar was approaching slowly but surely and soon he stood towering above us and glaring at our bit of cheese. We could hear a gurgling in his throat. He was choking with rage so that at first he was unable to utter a single word. But then he coughed and cleared his throat.

"Look at this pair of young men," he yelled. "They haven't a drop of decency left in them. Just look at the hurry they're in to devour their cheese so that not a quarter, I do not say a half, mind you, would they give to a poor, miserable old man."

Bagritsky rose, took up an attitude with one hand pressed to his heart. When all eyes were turned upon him he began reciting softly and pathetically in a quivering voice full of tragedy:

Friend of mine, brother of mine, my weary suffering brother,

Whoever thou art, despair not!

The beggar, after he had listened to a few more lines, stood transfixed, quailed and grew deathly pale. At the words "Trust, there will come the day when Baal shall perish!" he turned on his heel and upsetting a chair on his way made for the door with shaky knees.

"See!" said Bagritsky quite earnestly to the people in the tea-house. "Even Odessa's most hard-boiled beggar can't bear to hear Nadson."*

The whole tea-house shook with laughter.

Bagritsky spent days on end catching birds with a net in the steppes beyond the Firth of Sukhoi.

In Bagritsky's room in Moldavanka Street with its whitewashed walls and ceiling there hung dozens of cages containing grubby little birds. Of these he was extremely proud, particularly of what he considered rare specimens of the lark but which really were ordinary steppe larks as drab and tousled as the rest of the feathered creatures. The husks from the grains which the birds pecked at kept falling on the heads of Bagritsky's visitors. The poet spent his last coppers to feed them.

Odessa's newspapers paid Bagritsky a pittance for his fine verses—about fifty rubles for a poem, poems which several years later became so popular, particularly with

---

* Russian poet (1862-1887) known for his pessimistic verses.—*Tr.*

the youth, that they were on everyone's lips. Bagritsky, however, was certain that he was getting a fair price. He had no idea of his own worth and was very impractical. On his first visit to Moscow he never went to interview a publisher without taking a friend along "to break the ice." And the friend would do most of the talking while Bagritsky did little else but sit around and smile.

When he arrived in Moscow he came to stay with me, in the basement in Obidensky Street where I lived. He warned me: "Don't expect me ever to be out." And indeed during the month that he spent with me, he went to town only twice. The rest of the time he spent sitting Turkish fashion on the couch, coughing and choking with asthma. The couch around him was littered with books, manuscripts brought to him by various poets and empty cigarette packets on which he wrote down his own verses. Now and then he lost one of the packets, felt disappointed for a while, and then forgot all about it.

In this way he spent a whole month during which he never ceased admiring Selvinsky's poetry, relating the most implausible stories about himself and talking to the "literary boys," his fellow-Odessites, who flocked to see him as soon as they learned that he was in the capital.

When later he came to live in Moscow for good he got himself huge bowls with fishes to take the place of the bird-cage, making his room look like a submarine world. And here, too, he spent hours sitting on his couch, day-dreaming and staring absent-mindedly at the fishes.

His fish bowls reminded me of the bottom of the sea as we observed it from Odessa's breakwater. There were the swaying stalks of silvery seaweeds and the slowly drifting flouncy blue jelly-fish, cutting the sea water with their jerks.

It seems to me that Bagritsky had made a mistake by taking up permanent residence in Moscow. He should never have abandoned the south, the sea, and Odessa, and the Odessa food he was accustomed to—egg-plants, tomatoes, cheese and fresh mackerel. The south, the heat of the yellow limestone out of which most of Odessa was built, the smell of wormwood, brine, acacias and the surf were in his blood.

He died early without really having come to his own as a poet, and not ready, as he used to say, to scale more of the great heights of poetry.

His bier was followed by a squadron of cavalry, the granite-paved road ringing with the clatter of horses' hoofs. His poems, such as "Meditations about Opanas" and "Kotovsky's Steed" had the broad reach of the steppes. And as he was being borne on his last journey, his poetry—heir of *The Lay of Igor's Host*, of Taras Shevchenko, pungent as the smell of steppe-grass, sun-tanned as a beach beauty, and bracing as the fresh breeze that blows over the Black Sea which he loved so dearly— seemed to be marching by.

THE ART OF PERCEIVING THE WORLD

> "Painting teaches us to look and to perceive. (These are two different things, rarely identical.) And that is why painting helps to keep alive that unadulterated sense of perceiving things which is possessed by children!"
>
> ALEXANDER BLOK

here are indisputable truths that only too often remain hidden away and ineffectual because in our great indolence or ignorance we overlook them.

One of these truths is that knowledge of all the sister arts, such as poetry, painting, architecture, sculpture and music, will help to enrich the spiritual outlook of the prose writer and lend greater vigour to his writing. The play of lights and the tints in painting, the refreshing vocabulary of poetry, the harmony of architectural lines, the direct appeal of sculpture, the principles of music are all treasures added to prose, her complementary colours, as it were.

I do not believe writers who say that poetry or painting have no deep appeal for them. I think they must be either boors or they possess sluggish and arrogant minds.

The writer must not spurn anything that will help to broaden his vision of the world, if, of course, he regards himself not as a mere craftsman, but as a creator, not as a Philistine to whom writing is merely a stepping-stone to a life of comfort but as a true artist bent on giving something new and worthwhile to the world.

Often, after reading a story or a novel, and a long one at that, nothing remains in the mind, except irritation at the stupid, insipid hustling of the drab characters the author portrayed. Painfully one tries to form a picture of them, but in vain because the writer had not endowed any of them with a single life-like trait. And the background against which the action takes place is vague and amorphous, having neither colour nor light, with but the names of things, but the things themselves not really *seen* by the author and therefore not *shown* to the reader.

Books, often those dealing with contemporary life, are hopelessly puerile, written with an affected optimism. The tediousness of such books is due as much to the author's inability to *perceive* and *see* things, as to his emotional shallowness.

Reading such books is like being locked up in a dusty, stuffy chamber with the windows sealed. One longs to smash the windows open and feel the gusts of wind, hear the patter of the rain, the cries of children, the whistling of passing locomotives, see the gleam of wet pavements. And let life with its array of light, colour and sound burst in.

We have published quite a few books which seem to have been written by blind authors. Yet they are meant for a public which is not blind at all—hence the stupidity of letting such books see light.

To perceive one has not only to look around but to learn to see. And this can be achieved only if one loves his land and his people. Blurred vision and colourless prose are only too often the result of the writer's cold-bloodedness, a sure symptom of callousness. Sometimes it may be merely want of skill or lack of culture. This can be remedied.

How to *see,* how to perceive light and colour is something we can learn from painters. They can see better than we do. And they are better trained to remember what they see.

"You see things dimly and crudely," said a painter to me when I had just begun printing my stories. "Judging by what I've read by you, you see only the primary colours and the sharp lines, all your in-between shades and tints are a monotonous blur."

"There's nothing I can do about it, it's the sort of eye I've got," I said in self-defence.

"Nonsense, a good eye comes with training," the painter assured me. "You can learn to see colour the way we painters do. Keep your eye at work. Try for a month or two to look at things and people in trams, in buses, everywhere with the idea that you must paint them in colours. And you will soon be convinced that previously you had not seen a tenth part of what you see now in the faces around you. And in two months you will learn to see colour without any strain on your part at all."

I took the painter's advice and, true enough, people and things appeared in a far more interesting light than previously when I took stock of them hastily and sketchily. And with bitter regret I thought of the time I had wasted in the past. All the wonderful things I could have really *seen* and which I had missed *seeing,* gone for ever!

Thus my first important lesson in seeing things was given to me by a painter. The second—also by a painter—was something of an object lesson.

One autumn I travelled from Moscow to Leningrad not

by the usual route through Kalinin and Bologoye but via Kalyazin and Khvoinaya from the Savyolovsky Station. Though it takes longer by the second route, the traveller with an eye for scenery will enjoy it more for it passes through woodlands and through sparsely populated country.

My fellow-passenger in the train was a little man with narrow lively eyes. His clothes looked baggy and his luggage—a big box of paints and rolls of canvas—did not leave me in any doubt as to his occupation. I soon learned that he was bound for the country round Tikhvin (a little town midway between Moscow and Leningrad). There he would live in the woods with a forester he knew and paint the autumnal landscape.

"And why must you go to a far-off place like Tikhvin?" I asked.

"There is a spot there that I particularly want to paint," he told me trustingly. "You won't find another like it anywhere in the world. It's a pure aspen grove with a fir only here and there. And no tree is as beautiful as the asp in autumn. Its leaves are tinted a clear purple, lemon-yellow, mauve and even black with gold dots. They glow magnificently in the sun. I'll paint till winter there and then go up to the Gulf of Finland. There the hoar-frost is quite peculiar, not like anywhere else in Russia."

I suggested in jest that he could furnish his fellow-artists with some fine itineraries of the best scenery for painting in the land.

"I could do that easily," he replied in earnest. "But the idea is not so good as it sounds. It'll only draw everybody to some chosen spots, whereas each should do his own beauty hunting. That brings much better results."

"Why?"

"Wider coverage. And there is so much natural beauty in Russia that it can keep painters busy painting for another few thousand years. But," he added with a note of alarm in his voice, "man is working havoc with nature and destroying its beauties. The beauty of the earth is a sacred thing, a great thing in the life of society. It is one of our ultimate goals. I don't know about you but I'm convinced of it. And I can't call a man progressive unless he understands it."

In the afternoon I fell asleep but was presently awakened by the painter.

"I couldn't let you miss this," he said apologetically. "Look out of the window and you'll see that wonderful phenomenon—a thunder-storm in late September."

I glanced out of the window and saw a huge, straggly thunder-cloud drifting low from the south. It obscured half of the sky and swayed beneath the flashes of lightning.

"Good God! What a wealth of tints!" cried the painter. "And the play of lights, even Levitan couldn't paint it."

"What lights?" I asked.

"Where are you looking?" he cried despairingly. "Look the other way. The forest you see is black and dense because the thunder-cloud has thrown its shadow upon it. But farther—see the pale yellow and green spots—they are from the sunbeams breaking through the clouds. And still farther away the whole forest is bathed in sunlight, as though cast in red gold. It is like a wall wrought in gilt patterns—or like one of those huge kerchiefs embroidered with gold thread by the women in Tikhvin. And turn your eye to the belt of fir-trees, they're nearer to us. Do you see the bronze gleam, that's from the reflection cast by the gold wall of woods. Reflected light! It is very difficult to paint it because you must avoid overtones, and not miss the very delicate shadows and faint tints scattered here and there. The scene needs a very steady and confident hand."

The painter then looked at me and laughed with delight.

"The reflected lights of the autumnal woods are marvellous in the effects they produce. They've set ablaze our whole compartment. And your face, too, is all lighted up. I'd like to paint you that way. But the light will be gone in a moment."

"But that is the business of the artist," I said, "to capture the momentary and make it live through the ages."

"Yes, we try to do this," he replied. "When the momentary does not catch us unawares, as it has done now. And the painter, of course, should always have his paints, canvas and brushes with him. You writers here have an advantage over us. Your colours are locked up in your memory. Look at the rapid change of scene, the woods aflame one minute and plunged into darkness the next."

Tattered clouds sailed so precipitously in front of the thunder-cloud that they produced the strangest medley of colour, scarlet, russet and gold, malachite, purple and dark blue, all blended in the panorama of the distant woods. Now and then sunbeams broke through the dark clouds lighting up a birch here and there, making them one by one flare up and go out like flames in gold torches. The wind bringing the storm on its crest blew in gusts and added even greater confusion to the strange mingling of colours.

"What a sky!" cried the painter. "Just look what's going on over there!"

I turned to look and saw the thunder-cloud whirling in wreaths of dark ashy mist and drifting lower and lower. It was all the colour of slate except where the flashes of lightning made it gape with ominous yellow gashes, dark blue caverns, meandering cracks, all lighted from within by a vague pink light. Each streak of lightning left a smouldering copper flame in its wake. And nearer to the earth, between the dark cloud and the woods, the rain was already coming down in heavy sheets.

"What do you think of it!" cried the excited painter. "It is not often that you can see anything so magnificent."

We kept changing our position, now looking out of the window in our compartment, now out of the one in the corridor, the wind-blown curtains intensifying the impression of flickering lights.

The downpour grew heavier and the attendant quickly shut the windows. Slanting threads of rain ran down the window-panes. It grew dark and only in the distance where the earth met the sky a strip of gilded forest gleamed through the rainy sheet.

"Will you remember anything of what we have seen?" asked the painter.

"A thing or two."

"So will I, a thing or two," said he with regret. "The rain will pass and the colours will be more pronounced. The sun will play on the wet foliage and the tree trunks. By the way, it's a good idea to study lighting effects on a cloudy day—before rain, during rain and after rain. They're so different. The wet foliage imparts to the air a faint glimmer, greyish, soft and warm. To study colours and lighting effects in general is a great delight. I would not change my profession for anything in the world."

In the night the painter alighted at a small station. I had gone out on the platform to say good-bye to him in the flickering light of an oil lantern. The engine was puffing for all it was worth.

I now envied the painter and felt annoyed that various matters made it necessary for me to continue my journey, and prevented me from stopping at least for a few days and enjoying the beauties of this northern country where every twig of heather inspired thoughts enough to fill pages and pages of poetic prose.

I was sorry to think then that like all people in the world, I could not follow the impulses of my heart, prevented by one thing or another that brooked no delay.

The tints and play of light in nature are not merely to be observed. They must be experienced, for in art only that which has taken root in the heart of the artist is of any use.

Painting will help develop in the writer an understanding and fondness for colour and light. Besides the painter often sees things which entirely escape our vision. Only when we perceive these things in his pictures do we wonder why we hadn't noticed them before.

Claude Monet, the French artist, painted Westminster Abbey on one of London's foggy days. Its Gothic contours are dimly visible in the enveloping mist. The picture is a masterpiece.

When it was exhibited in London it created quite a stir. The Londoners were amazed to find that Monet had painted the fog a crimson colour. Whoever heard of a fog being anything but grey? The public was indignant at Monet's boldness. But when the Londoners left the salon and went out into the streets and looked closely at the fog, they realized that there were, indeed, crimson tints in it. They began to seek for an explanation and soon all agreed that the smoke of London's factories and the large number of red brick houses in the city were responsible for it.

But whatever the explanation, Monet taught Londoners to see the fog as he had seen it and became known as the "creator of the London fog."

In the same way, after seeing Levitan's picture *Eternal Peace*, I realized that a cloudy day is rich in hues. Previously it had been all one dull colour to me and I thought it made the world look so dreary because it blotted out all tints and cast a dismal veil over everything.

But Levitan was able to divine in that dreariness a majestic and solemn beauty with many pure tints. Ever since overcast skies have ceased to depress me. I have learned to love the clear air, the nipping cold, the leaden rippling of the river, and the low drifting skies of a cloudy day. Besides, inclement weather makes one appreciate the simple boons of life in the country—a warm peasant hut, the fire in a Russian stove, the humming of the samovar, the bed of hay with a homespun cover over it, laid out for you on the floor of the hut, the lulling patter of the rain and the sweet drowsiness it brings.

Almost every painter of any period or school has the power to reveal to us new important features in his own peculiar perception of reality.

I have had the good fortune to visit the Dresden gallery a number of times. Apart from Raphael's *Sistine Madonna*, I have found there scores of pictures by Old Masters from which it is impossible to tear oneself away. I could spend hours, even whole days looking at them. And the longer I looked the more impressed I was. Indeed, I was moved to tears because these canvases represented the height of human genius, the peerlessness of the human spirit and they appealed to the best and noblest in me.

Contemplation of the beautiful stirs and purifies; like the freshness of the air and wind, the breath of the blossoming land, of the nocturnal sky, as well as tears shed for love, it expands and ennobles our hearts.

I should like to say a few words about the Impressionists. We must be grateful to the Impressionists for having made us more keenly aware of the sunlight. They painted in the open air and sometimes laid deliberate emphasis on colour, with the result that all things on their canvases were bathed in a glow of radiant light. There was a festive air about their pictures. And by the pictures they painted they have added to the sum total of human joys.

The Impressionists have never been popular in our country. Yet I think there is much we can learn from them and other representatives of the French schools of painting. To turn our backs on them, chiefly because they gave little attention to subject-matter, or chose trifling subjects not to our taste is to take a deliberately narrow view of things. It would be just as ridiculous to denounce the *Sistine Madonna* because this great masterpiece deals with a religious subject. Nobody would think of doing such a thing in our country. Yet the Impressionists have continually been a target. What harm can there be in recognizing the diverse Picasso, or such painters as Matisse, van Gogh or Gaugin and learning what we can from them? Certainly, none.

After my encounter with the painter in the train I arrived in Leningrad—to feast my gaze yet another time on the stately, well-proportioned buildings in its squares. These buildings presented an architectural riddle to me which I had long tried to solve: how, though of unimposing size, were they able to give the impression of such greatness and magnificence? For example, there is the Building of the General Staff facing the Winter Palace. It is no more than four storeys in height, yet as a building it is more significant and impressive-looking than some very tall and big buildings in Moscow.

The reason for this, I think, is the wonderful harmony of its proportions and the scant use of decoration. On scrutinizing the buildings closely one can't help thinking that good taste is above all a sense of proportion.

I have a feeling that the laws that govern proportion in architecture, the absence of everything superfluous, few ornaments, the kind of simplicity which helps to bring out the beauty of each line and delight the eye with it—all have direct bearing on prose.

A writer able to appreciate the classical severity of architectural forms will co-ordinate all the parts of his story in a well-knit pattern, avoiding heaviness and awkwardness in its arrangement as well as too frequent use of flowery language, the ornaments that devitalize prose.

The structure of a work of prose must be brought to a state that would permit of no deletion or addition without violating the sense and course of events.

In Leningrad, as was my custom, I spent most of my time in the Russian Museum and at the Hermitage.

The light in the halls of the Hermitage, slightly dim, and tinged by dark gold, seemed sacred to me. I worshipped the Hermitage as the greatest shrine of human genius. Even in my early boyhood a visit to the Hermitage exalted me. I rejoiced to think what greatness and goodness the human heart and mind can conceive.

On my first visits to this great treasure house of art I felt quite lost in the midst of all its paintings. The wealth and beauty of colour made my head swim. To relax a little and get my bearings I would go to the hall where sculptures were exhibited. I spent much time there and the longer I looked at the old Greek statues or at Canova's strangely smiling women, the better I understood how strongly these sculptures appealed to our sense of beauty. The sentiments they inspired would lead us, I know, to the real dawn of humanity when poetry shall reign supreme in our hearts and the social order towards which we march through years of labour, trial and ordeal will be founded on the beauty of justice, the beauty of the mind, of the heart, of human relationships and of the human body.

We are marching towards a golden age. It will come. It is only to be regretted that we of the present generation shall not live to see it, yet we can feel its refreshing breath and this makes us happy.

It is a well-known fact that Heine had spent hours sitting and weeping in front of the statue of Venus de Milo in the Louvre.

Why did he weep? For blighted genius? Or because the path to self-fulfilment is long and thorny? Or that he, Heine, who had given to his readers so much of the venom and sparkle of his mind, would never reach the goal of perfection?

The emotional power of sculpture is great. It brings with it an inner light without which an advanced art, and a powerful literature, particularly such as we must have in our country, are inconceivable.

Before discussing the influence of poetry upon prose I wish to say a few words about the musical quality in writing, for music and poetry are often inseparable. I shall speak of music briefly, only touching upon rhythm and the music of prose.

Well-written prose always has its own peculiar rhythm. Good rhythm in prose requires such an arrangement of words in the sentence that the thought is at once and without the least strain grasped by the reader. Chekhov stressed this when he wrote to Gorky that "fiction must instantaneously reach the reader's mind."

The reader must not begin reshuffling the words in a piece of writing so as to grasp the meaning better. The rhythm must be "in character" with the piece. An unbroken easy-flowing, well-balanced rhythm will help the writer to keep the unflagging interest of the reader, and will make the reader enter into the thoughts and feelings of the writer.

I do not think that rhythm in prose can ever be achieved artificially. Rhythm depends on the writer's talent and feeling for language and his "ear for words." An ear for words is in some measure connected with an ear for music, and also the writer's love and understanding of poetry.

Poetry contributes greatly to the richness of language. It possesses an almost uncanny power of imparting to words an elemental, virginal freshness. Words that through frequent use and abuse have become dry commonplaces no longer suggesting anything vital to us are given a new lease on life by the poet. In a line of poetry they begin to sparkle, ring and smell sweet.

There are two ways of revitalizing a hackneyed word that has become devalued. Firstly, by giving a new beauty to its sound. Poetry is in a better position to accomplish this than prose. That is why the words in a song or a poem have greater power to move us than the same words occurring in prose. Secondly, even a word which has grown trite, when appearing in a line of verse, will gain in significance in combination with other words. And lastly, poetry is rich in alliteration. This is one of its most precious qualities. And prose too has its right to alliteration.

But perhaps what it is most important for the prose writer to realize is that consummate prose is really nothing more or less than genuine poetry.

Lermontov's *Taman* and Pushkin's *Captain's Daughter* prove, according to Chekhov, how closely akin Russian prose was to Russian verse.

"Where is the border-line between prose and poetry, I shall never know," Tolstoi ardently declares in his *Youth Diary:*

"Why are poetry and prose so closely linked, and happiness and unhappiness?" he goes on to ask. "How must one live? Try all at once to blend poetry with prose or delight in one and later let oneself fall under the sway of the other. There is a side to dreams which is superior to reality and in reality a side which is superior to dreams. Complete happiness would be in uniting the two."

In these words, though penned in haste, there is a correct thought: the summits of literature and true perfection can be reached only in an organic integration of poetry and prose, or, to be exact, in saturating prose with the essence of poetry with its well-springs, its pure breath, the alluring power of its beauty.

IN A LORRY

I was riding in an army lorry from Rybnitsy-on-Dniester to Tiraspol, in July 1941, when the Nazis were invading the Soviet Union. I sat in front at the side of the driver, who hardly spoke a word.

Clouds of brown, sun-baked dust rose from under the wheels. Everything around us—the peasant huts, the sunflowers, the acacias and the seared grass—was covered with gritty dust. Overhead in a colourless sky the sun was obscured by a haze. In our aluminium flasks the water was hot and smelt of rubber. From across the Dniester came the roar of guns.

Several young lieutenants seated in the lorry would now and then bang with their fists on the top over the driver's seat and shout: "Air-raid!" The driver would bring the lorry to an abrupt halt, we would jump out, run a little distance and drop face downwards on the ground while German Messerschmidts droned and swooped viciously overhead.

On spotting us, the Germans would open fire. Fortunately, we escaped being hit during that long ride, the bullets only churning the dust. When the Messerschmidts were gone, we felt our bodies burning with heat from long contact with the sun-scorched ground, a drumming in the head and a terrible thirst.

"What are you thinking about lying like that on the ground? Your home?" the driver asked me unexpectedly after one of the attacks.

"I suppose so," I replied.

"Same here," he said and paused. "I think of the woods at Kostroma. That's my home. If I come through this I'll go there and get a forester's job; I'll take along the wife, she's quiet and nice to look at, and my daughter. Thinking of it all affects the heart, and that's bad for a driver."

"And I think of the woods I love," I replied.

"Are yours beautiful?" asked the driver.

"I should think so!"

The driver pulled his army cap lower over his forehead and began to drive at a greater speed.

I never thought so much of the places I loved best as on the battle-fields. I would be waiting for the night to come and then give myself up wholly to reverie. I would lie in a lorry, covered by my greatcoat. Inhaling the pine-scented air, I would say to myself: "Today I shall stroll down to the Black Lake and tomorrow, if I'm still alive, I'll go down to the River Pra or Trebutino." And my heart would miss a beat as I thought of the pleasure that even a purely imaginary outing into the woods, to the lake or to the river, gave me.

And once as I lay thus, covered by my greatcoat, I reconstructed in my mind a very accurate picture of the road through the woods that led to the lake. It seemed to me then that there was no greater happiness on earth than seeing once more these places, forgetting all your troubles and sorrows and listening to the carefree beating of your heart.

I imagined myself early in the morning leaving the peasant cottage, in which I happened to be staying the night and sallying forth into the village streets lined by old huts, on the window-sills of which were usually rows of tin cans with flaming flower plants growing in them. Near the well, where all day long barefooted young girls in faded calico frocks chatted as they rattled their buckets, I knew I had to turn into a side-street. Here in the last house lived the proudest cock for miles and miles around, his plumage as bright as glowing coals in a fire. Where the row of cottages ended was a narrow-gauge railway track stretching into the outlying woods. On its bank grew flowers quite different from those of the surrounding country. And nowhere was there such an abundance of chicory as along this sun-baked track. Farther down was what at first appeared to be a trackless copse of pine saplings. As I passed it I knew the pine needles would prick me and gluey spots of resin would stain my fingers.

I could see tall, dry grass growing in the sandy soil of the wood. The blades of grass were grey in the middle and dark green at the edges and very sharp. There would also be an abundance of yellow immortelles, strongly scented wild carnations with pink spots on their curly white petals and a host of mushrooms nestling under the trees.

Beyond the copse was a wood with tall trees, fringed by a grassy path. I thought of how pleasant it was to lie down to rest here under a spreading pine-tree. The air would feel fresh and cool after the closeness of the copse. I could lie for hours gazing up into the sky and feeling the coolness of the earth through my shirt. I would feel wonderfully at peace with the world, watching the endless drifting of the clouds with their shining, frayed edges, and feeling a drowsiness come upon me. Lying like this I would recall Bryusov's verses:

> To be alone, at liberty
> Amid the solemn quiet of the fields so vast,
> To walk your road in freedom and infinity
> Without a future or a past.
> To gather flowers of a fleeting bloom,
> To drink in sun-rays like a love refrain,
> To fall and die and vanish in the gloom,
> And come to life, without regret or joy, again...

There is in those verses—though death is mentioned in them—so much of the fullness of life, that they make you long even more to lie in the woods and look into the sky.

Then to rise—and follow the trail running through an ancient pine-wood over rolling sandy hills, undulating like huge waves across the surf. These hills were remains of the ice-age. On the hilltops grew hosts of bluebells and at the foot of the hills were carpets of bracken with leaves covered on the inside with spores resembling reddish specks of dust. How well I saw in my mind's eye the woodlands on the hillsides, bathed in sunlight—a long strip of forest beyond which were fields of ripening grain shimmering and swaying in the wind. And then the fields again extended into a dense pine-forest. Clouds floating above the fields seemed particularly grand and imposing—perhaps because here you got such a far-flung view of the sky.

I could see myself crossing the fields along a path overgrown with burdock, in between the patches of grain, with firm little bluebells peeping through the grass here and there.

So far the picture I saw in my mind but vaguely suggested the real beauty of the woodlands as I knew it.

Going into the woods was like losing oneself in a huge, shady cathedral. At first you go along the path past the pond which was covered with a green carpet of duck-weed, the pond itself with the carps champing the sea-weed; and farther was a small coppice of birch draped in green velvety moss and smelling of fallen leaves from the previous autumn.

I resumed my reveries and found myself transported to a little spot in the coppice which always made my heart leap with joy.

I thought of all this in the dead of night. A railway station not far away was being bombed and I could hear the blasts. When they died down the timid chirping of the cicada reached my ears. Frightened by the explosion they hummed very softly. I watched the descent of a blue star and wondered: will there be an explosion? But the star faded out silently and seemed almost to touch the earth. I thought of the great distance that lay between me and the places I loved so dearly. There, too, it was night. But a different night—silent, resplendent in the brilliance of its peaceful constellations, smelling not of petrol and explosive but of forest pools and juniper.

Then I passed through the coppice and was walking up the road that rose steeply to a sandy height. The damp lowlands were left behind but a light breeze still carried their freshness to me to the hot stuffy woods. On the height I had my second siesta. I sat down on the hot ground. Everything around was dry and warm to the touch—the old hollow pine cones, the young pine bark, every little twig, and the tree-trunks, decayed to the pith. Even the tiny petals of the wild strawber-ry bushes were warm. Bits of tree-stumps broke off easily and the rotted wood crumbled into dust in your hand.

It was a sultry and peaceful day with all of summer's ripeness.

Little dragon-flies with their tiny red wings were asleep on the tree-stumps. Bumble-bees weighed down the purplish petals of the woodland flowers as they alighted on them.

I could see myself checking my whereabouts on a map of my own making. Another eight kilometres to go before I would reach the Black Lake.

The landmarks I went by were on the map—a dry birch by the road, a milepost, a patch of brushwood, an ant-hill, a dip with hosts of forget-me-nots and then a pine-tree with the initial letter of "Lake" carved on its bark. At the pine-tree one turned into the wood. There one was guided by notches made on the trees in 1932, gradually effaced by resin and renewed every year. I remembered that whenever I would come across a notch I would stop and touch the hard amber-like resin, sometimes breaking off a piece and examining the yellow flames of sunlight playing in it.

On the way to the lake the forest was cut up by deep gullies—most likely dried-up lakes—with a dense growth of alder bushes that made them practically impassable. Then there was an ascent through thickets of juniper with withered blackberries. And finally the last landmark—a pair of dry bast sandals, suspended from a pine branch. After a narrow glade and a steep incline the forest came to an end. Below were dried up marshes covered with brushwood. Here I could make my last stop. It would be after midday and there would be a humming as though there were swarms of bees and the treetops would sway at the faintest stir of wind.

One and a half more miles to go and there was the Black Lake, a kingdom of dark waters, snags and huge yellow water-lilies. I knew I had to watch my step as I walked through the deep moss, for here and there were jagged birch stumps and I could easily stumble and bruise myself. The air was close and mouldy and the black peat-bog water squelched under your feet. And the saplings swayed and shook at every step you took. The peat was about a yard deep and you tried not to think that beneath it was deep water—a subterranean lake they said, with pikes in it as black as coal. The shores of the lake were somewhat more elevated than the surrounding country so that the moss was drier. Still you couldn't stand long in one place without your feet sinking in deeper all the time and a puddle being formed around you.

It was best to emerge on the shore of the lake in the last hour of twilight when everything around—the faint gleam of the water as well as that of the first stars appearing in the heavens, the greying sky, the motionless treetops—seemed to merge with the quivering tranquillity as though born of it. And now that I had reached my destination I could sit down, light a fire, listen to the crackling of the twigs and reflect on how remarkably delicious life was—if one harboured no fears and lived in all the fullness of one's heart.

Thus in my musings I roamed first through the woods, then along the Neva embankments in Leningrad or among the hills, blue with flowering flax, in the rugged country around Pskov and through many other places.

I now thought of these places with a deep ache in my heart as though they were lost to me for ever and this made them seem to me perhaps far more beautiful than they really were. I wondered why I had not felt so poignantly about them before and realized that distance had, indeed, enhanced the beauty of the scenes I knew so well. They had now sunk deeper than ever into my consciousness, every bit of landscape falling into place, like notes blending into the harmony of music.

To fully appreciate the beauties of Nature we must find in it moods akin to our own, to blend with our frame of mind, the love we feel, our joys and sorrows. Then the freshness of the morning will recall to us the lovelight in the eyes of our beloved and the measured rustling of the woods, the beat of our own lives. Descriptions of nature are neither an appendage to prose nor an ornament. They should be like heaps of rain-wet leaves into which we could bury our faces and feel their wonderful coolness and fragrance.

In other words nature must be loved and that love, like any other love, will find true ways to express itself with the greatest force.

A WORD TO MYSELF

now finish my first book of notes on literature in the making with a feeling that what
I have said here is but an infinitesimal part
of what must be said on this absorbing
subject. Some of the problems that I hope
to touch upon in future books of this character are—the aesthetic side of our literature, its great
significance as a literature which must help mould the
new man, a being rich and noble in mind and heart, subject-matter, humour, imagery and character delineation,
changes in the Russian language, the popular character
of literature, romanticism, good taste, how to edit a manuscript—and heaps of other problems.

Working on this book has been in the nature of a journey through a little-known land where at every step
new vistas and new roads opened, leading one knew not
where but having in store many surprises which give food
for thought. To get some idea, vague and sketchy perhaps, of this tangle of roads, the land must be further ex-
plored and the journey continued.

ПАУСТОВСКИЙ

ЗОЛОТАЯ РОЗА

Printed in the Union of Soviet Socialist Republics